CREATE YOUR COLLEGE SUCCESS

Activities and Exercises for Students

Robert A. Friday, Ph.D.

Designer/Trainer, New Student Seminar Program
Assistant Professor, Communication
Duquesne University

Wadsworth Publishing Company
Belmont, California
A Division of Wadsworth, Inc.

PRODUCTION EDITOR Leland Moss
DESIGNER Carolyn Deacy
EDITORIAL ASSISTANT Sharon Wallach
PRINT BUYER Barbara Britton
COPY EDITOR Anne Montague
COVER Carolyn Deacy
SIGNING REPRESENTATIVE Mike Sugarman

Printed in the United States of America   49

1 2 3 4 5 6 7 8 9 10—92 91 90 89 88

Library of Congress Cataloging-in-Publication Data

Friday, Robert A.
    Create your college success / Robert A. Friday.
        p.   cm.
    ISBN 0-534-09318-3
    1. College student orientation—United States.   I. Title.
LB2343.32.F75   1988
378'.198—dc19   87-35191
                                                                 CIP

To James C. Friday and Phyllis B. Friday, my parents, for sitting me down and persuading me to become a freshman. To Sharon Friday, my loving wife, who encourages me to remain a freshman in discovery and enthusiasm, and who spent hours proofreading, offering countless valuable insights, suggestions, and above all, inspiration. To these people this volume is dedicated.

A special thanks to Barbara Galderise, director of health services, Duquesne University, who assisted in the research of several chapters, and Professor Ruth Biro, School of Education, who contributed to the library discovery exercises. Also thanks to Ron Anderson, J. Patrick Boyle, James Cox, Jay Johnston, Debra Li-coto-Meiman, Jack Nelson, Virginia Tomlinson, Pat Watt, and Irene Wolf, all of whom contributed through their work to the success of the New Student Seminar at Duquesne and thereby to this book.

Thanks to Robert and Carole Ussack, my father-in-law and mother-in-law, who love big sister Gillian and little Andrew, for freeing my hands for typing.

To the thousands of students who have shared their problems, hopes, and dreams with me for teaching me how to help them.

And, of course, a very special thanks to John N. Gardner and A. Jerome Jewler, whose generous and inspired collaboration is changing the way freshmen everywhere approach personal and intellectual growth.

❖ Contents ❖

❖ Introduction ❖

At the request of the author, we're pleased to introduce this book with some words of advice for those of you who are about to enter the wonderful, challenging, frustrating, rewarding, unexpected, exciting, and always fascinating world of what we professors call "higher education" and you call "college."

Quite simply, the advice is to get on with the business of being in college by giving college everything you've got. If you don't know quite how to do that (and few people come equipped with this knowledge as freshmen), you're going to appreciate what this book can do to help. Because it isn't merely a book to be read and remembered; it's a book that asks you to give of yourself in return.

For learning "college" isn't exactly like studying history. Experience is the key to learning how to make the most of your college years, and experience is what you'll find within these pages in the form of one activity after another designed to help you realize the breadth and depth of the college experience.

To use an example, take the group activity called "The Social Problem" that appears on page 125. Its purpose is to indicate that each of us has his or her own personal system of values and that each of us therefore has the right to disagree, providing we don't expect everyone else to agree with us. To state this simply seems obvious; but experiencing value decisions in "The Social Problem" and other similar exercises can be both revealing and instructive to those who participate—and teaches each participant to be tolerant of differing attitudes within the group, even if he or she is not in agreement with those attitudes.

So it goes with the other critical areas covered in this extensive collection, areas such as social and intellectual development, physical and spiritual development, and emotional and vocational development. What's even more intriguing about these exercises is that many of them can work whether you undertake them on your own or as part of a group of students in a class, a club, or simply as an extracurricular activity.

If you use this book in conjunction with one of our books (*College Is Only the Beginning* or *Step by Step to College Success*), you will find that, whereas our books provide important information and food for thought on succeeding in college, this book gives you a chance to express those ideas in highly active and interactive ways. You might even say the three of us planned it that way.

We commend Bob for his incredible talent in creating a large group of exercises, gathering others from many different sources, and weaving them into a work that not only provides valuable information but employs creative exercises that allow the reader to absorb and actively use that information in so many unforgettable ways.

Enjoy the book. Work at the exercises. Have fun while you're doing them. We can assure you that we did.

John N. Gardner
A. Jerome Jewler

❖ Preface ❖

The Origin of This Book

When I began to design the New Student Seminar program at Duquesne University in 1985, I had already been following the work of John N. Gardner and A. Jerome Jewler for five years. What they were saying about the freshman year echoed what I had encountered every day during my seven years as an academic adviser at the University of Pittsburgh. The freshman is entering a new world that looks deceptively like the old high school situation with chalkboards, desks, teachers—and yet the pressure of making life-defining decisions affects each and every one.

When our New Student Seminar program was on the drawing board, Gardner and Jewler's *College Is Only the Beginning* was published. I was thrilled and relieved to find that the issues I wanted my staff to negotiate with our freshmen were discussed in one book . I adopted the book at once and for the first time in my life began a major project with half the work completed.

The second half of my task, as a professor of communication and a training consultant, was to develop Individual Exercises and activities to help my staff get away from the standard lecture format and into a process of discovery with the students. The New Student Seminar (or freshman seminar) is not a content course that presents so many facts and theories. The freshman brings his or her own agenda to this class. The faculty are there to help freshmen find answers to their problems; make sense out of confusion and fear; translate their dreams, skills, and values into an academic plan (often with career objectives); and create strategies for success. Above all, this process of discovery must involve the student and faculty in the development of meaningful relationships that will last a lifetime.

The instructor's manual and handouts that I produced for our first faculty training were designed as a supplement to *College Is Only the Beginning. Create Your College Success* is an expansion of the manual and handouts with the addition of **purpose, directions,** and **closure** for each Individual Exercise or Group Activity to help both freshmen and faculty create a learning experience that responds to the needs of the students. Similarly, this book builds on the direction taken by Gardner and Jewler in *Step by Step to College Success,* which is a distillation of their first book with the addition of some Individual Exercises.

Freshmen, This Is Your Discovery Book

The purpose of this book is to give you and your faculty a number of ways to investigate and build on the concepts and information put forth in *College Is Only the Beginning* (1985, 1989) and *Step by Step to College Success* (1987). The **Individual Exercises** and **Group Activities** are organized in chapters that conform to the order of *College Is Only the Beginning* (1989). An **Individual Exercise** is designed to be worked on by you alone, giving you a better understanding of a central aspect of the corresponding chapter in *College Is Only the Beginning* . A **Group Activity** is often designed to build upon the results of the preceding Individual Exercises; activities are creative ways to involve you with your peers in the themes espoused by Gardner and Jewler. Individual Exercises and Group Activities require you to: **(1)** write, speak, and think critically; **(2)** interact with and interview many people; **(3)** develop consensus in small groups; and **(4)** research problems. Through these various communication experiences, you should gain an understanding of the role that college can play in developing your future success and happiness.

A Personal Note to Freshmen

Use this book. Write in this book. Pull together your insights—combine them with the views of others. As you proceed, you will look back on old chapters and find that you are constructing your own map to college and career success. Keep this book. Follow your map. Years after graduation, you will look back on your moments of self-discovery as focal points for career and life decisions.

At times, your instructor may join the class in an Group Activity and let you direct the class. I encourage you to try directing an Group Activity and urge that everyone in the classroom offer support and cooperation. Such a task is not always easy, but the experience can be invaluable!

The Journal and You

Every chapter in this book concludes with a journal assignment devised to help you investigate your feelings, practice your writing, and integrate your new discoveries into your life. I urge you to buy or (as some students do) construct a notebook that can serve as your expressive space. Follow the journal assignments and explore your own experiences. The journal will help you clarify your feelings and impose your order on traditional first-year chaos. The journal will help you investigate your reactions to situations, to others, and to your own hopes and fears. I collect my students' journals several times during the term and give them written feedback on their entries. Your instructor may also do this. In the end, your journal will give you what it has given to thousands of freshmen: understanding. Put another way: experience + knowledge + reflection = understanding.

A Personal Note from a Freshman

When I entered college with the class of 1970, the furthest thing from my mind was becoming a college professor in communication—not to mention an international consultant specializing in the transfer of executives between Germany and the United States. And yet those two roles that I play can be traced to the strengths and interests that grew in me with each year of discovery. If I had had a freshman seminar, I feel that my path through painful years of self-examination and confusion in college would have included a more productive learning experience. My hope is that this book will give you the chance to define what you want to know, so that you don't just guide your choices with "shoulds" and "requirements that you take to get them out of the way."

Many freshmen administrators and faculty hold a new idea that we should empower freshmen—which reminds me of the words from the great German author Goethe: "Danger itself fosters the rescuing power." In entering college, you are plunging into a fast-moving stream of decision making and learning. I hope this book will help to empower you to make the decisions that are right for you.

Please note in the first two chapters I have included "Trivia Teasers." I welcome any students or faculty to send their trivia teasers to me so that I can include them in the next edition of this book. Finally, I would be grateful for your suggestions on any improvements for the next edition.

Robert A. Friday, Ph.D.
Freshman, 1966–

Freshman September

Where's my room;
Where's my space.
my home, my pet—
mom and dad—some familiar
place?

I miss my friends
and special things
while others carry on
—and sing—and dance
—and drink—and smoke
—and yell out windows:
"Last one to the bar buys
the beer!"

But I'm here.
—a tear
shedding in some other world,
some others' world.
I shed the former me
September shedding autumn tree.
Inward cry and quake—and
lie awake.
I fake—a smile and while
away the day—away the night.
To distant home from present
fright.

I don't want to be here!
I'm going home.
I'm gonna get out that suitcase
and duffel bag
and find some boxes and pack it all in.

My folks were wrong!
They'll just have to admit it.
They're going to see me take
a firm stand on this one.
'Cause the people here aren't friendly.

The teachers don't care.
The food's lousy.
The dorm's noisy
and crowded
and—and—everything!

I've got two hours before my roommate
come back from class.
I'll be gone—
and they'll be glad to see me go!
They'll put their junk in my space
and forget I ever existed—
and that's fine with me.
"Oh, hi guys. What are you doing
back early?"

"We were in orientation class."
"Our instructor said that all
freshmen experience culture shock,
homesickness, confusion, denial,
withdrawal, compensation, loneliness,
frustration, alienation, anomie,
depression, and bizarre behavior
of one form or another."

"You're kidding?!?"
"Do you guys feel all that?"

"Oh no—not us —but most freshmen
do."

"Yeah—I'll bet
—like those guys in the next room."

"Yeah—but our instructor said it
still could happen—you know
a delayed reaction.
So we're supposed to sit down
with our roommate and talk about our favorite things."

"You mean like pizza with
green peppers, mushrooms
and onions?"

"You're on!"

❖ Chapter 1 ❖

The Transition to College

Students entering college today have little in common with the freshmen of the first half of this century. Today's freshman classes include many more women, racial minorities, first-generation college students, international students, economically and culturally disadvantaged students, as well as other segments of our population. Although many freshmen still arrive at college directly from high school, more and more are "returning students" with advanced age, experience, and a set of needs very different from that of the 18-year-old freshman. Returning students will find specific advice and exercises for their transitional needs in Chapter 21 of this book. This chapter will focus more on the needs of the freshman who has entered college directly from high school.

As a freshman, you are joining a new society that is much different from high school. If you chose your college carefully, this new society will offer some resources that support the educational and career goals you have *at present*. I emphasize "at present" because most freshmen change majors several times before graduation. I urge you to leave yourself open to

1

the option of changing your mind. Beyond anything else, your new campus society is dedicated to changing your mind by introducing you to new ideas. Like a kid in a candy store, you will find yourself attracted to new delights during your college years. If you are like most freshmen, you will be torn between the economic need to declare a major and get on with your career and the basic human need to do things that are interesting to you. The advice that I give my freshmen is to do both.

As ideas and problems excite you, include them in your course selection and extracurricular activities. Watch your skills grow and your interests expand. Explore your new campus society to find out what options it can offer. The options include not only academic pursuits, but also a host of resources to support your college success. The exercises that follow will help you to discover your campus, beginning with the least obvious aspect: the rules of your new society.

Individual Exercise 1.1 *The Rules of Your Campus*

Purpose: This exercise is designed to help you to clarify the distinctions between high school and college. Although some differences may be clearly stated in your college's publication of rights and responsibilities of students, other rules may be more informal. Few faculty members are going to tell you when to start reviewing for midterms, when to start a research paper, or how much research is enough. Nor is anyone going to warn you about the pitfalls of new relationships—but they are there waiting for you. This exercise will help you adjust to your new college society.

When this individual exercise is completed, you will be ready to share your findings with your classmates in Group Activity 1.2.

Directions: You will find a questionnaire beginning on page 3 that focuses on two areas: the *academic* and the *social*. To complete the questionnaire, ask one or several upperclassmen these questions as well as others of your own. The best upperclassmen to interview would be those who are succeeding as students—those who make fairly good grades, are happy, and/or in a position of responsibility on campus: dorm assistant, student government member, *someone who knows the ropes*. You would do well to interview a resident for the resident section and a commuter for the commuter section. (**Trivia Teaser:** What is the origin of the metaphor "the ropes" and what does it imply about your student success? After you have given it some thought, see the end of the chapter.)

Note: As you proceed with your interview, write the responses in the space provided.

Questionnaire on the Hidden Rules and Ropes

Academics

1. What was your biggest academic adjustment in your transition from high school to

    college? _____

    _____

    _____

2. How has your college studying experience differed from high school studying?_____

    _____

    _____

3. What are the best courses (high school or college) you have taken and why were they

    good? _____

    _____

    _____

4. Who are the best faculty in your opinion? Why? _____

    _____

    _____

5. Are there usually study groups for difficult classes, and if so, how are they formed?

_____

_____

6. How can I find copies of old tests to use as study aids? _____

_____

_____

7. Where are the best places to study on campus between classes and in the evening?_____

_____

_____

8. When is your best study time? _____

_____

_____

9. When do you begin to study for midterms or finals? _____

_____

_____

Student Life

1. What do you do for fun on weekends? _____

_____

_____

2. Have you experienced any racial conflict during college, and if so, how did you resolve

   it? _____

   _____

   _____

3. What are the reputations of the various social groups on campus? _____

   _____

   _____

4. What are the best places to eat on or near campus? _____

   _____

   _____

5. What are the best ways to meet new people at college? _____

   _____

   _____

6. What negative social experiences have you or your friends had at college?_____

   _____

   _____

Residence (Dorm or Apartment)

1. Do you have any advice for getting along with a roommate? _____

   _____

   _____

2. What do you do if you can't get along with a roommate? _____

_____

_____

3. Who do you go to if you can't solve a problem in the dorm? _____

_____

_____

4. What should I do if a roommate wants to have a guest in the room when I want quiet or

privacy? _____

_____

_____

5. What are the typical problems of dorm life?_____

_____

_____

Commuting

1. What is the best way to keep in touch with commuter information? _____

_____

_____

2. Where are the best places to park?_____

_____

_____

3. Where do commuters hang out on campus? _____

_____

_____

4. What are some ways to get involved in campus life? _____

_____

_____

5. What are the typical problems of the commuter at this college?_____

_____

_____

Your Questions

If the questions that you would like answered are not in the questionnaire, write them in the space below and include them in your interview.

_____

_____

_____

_____

Closure: At the end of this exercise you should have had an informative session with at least one upperclassman. My hope is that you made at least one new contact in your new society. You also have some vital information that many students have to learn by trial and error. If your class does not do Group Activity 1.2, you should informally share your discoveries with several other freshmen in order to get a better view of what is in store for you, as well as to give yourself another opportunity to meet some of your fellow freshmen.

Group Activity 1.2 *Sharing the Unwritten Rules*

Purpose: In *College Is Only the Beginning*, Gardner and Jewler emphasize your need to understand the difference between high school and college, so that you can avoid a rude awakening. Things may look the same because you see chalkboards, books, and teachers. But professors are different from teachers, just as the rights and responsibilities of a college student are different from those of a high school student.

In Individual Exercise 1.1 you were directed to discover some of the unwritten rules and customs of your new college society. In this activity, the members of your freshman seminar can share their findings; you will get a pretty good preview of the unwritten codes of your college.

Directions: Sit in a circle. One member of the class should be in charge of calling on each student so that an orderly process can be maintained. This leader begins by asking who obtained valuable information in each area, beginning with Question 1 and proceeding through each student's own questions. The leader is to be sure that everyone has an opportunity to speak.

Closure: Generally this kind of activity produces a mixture of humor, good feelings, and valuable information. Be sure to make a note of any new details that you might want to remember in the future.

Group Activity 1.3 *Developing a Sense of Group*

Purpose: Your freshman seminar is a unique support group of your peers, whose life experiences are different from yours. As freshmen you are all joined in the same purpose: to improve your lives through learning. You are probably unaware of the feelings you have in common about your freshman experience. Discovering this common bond will bring you closer as a group. It will help you be more supportive of each other in your transition period.

Directions: Each student must quickly interview ten students in the freshman seminar. The two interviewing must agree on a positive anticipation or experience that they share and a negative fear or experience that they share in regard to their freshman experience thus far. When the shared experience is recognized, both should record it on the form that follows. For example, last year in our New Student Seminar most students expressed loneliness and fear as their strongest negative feeling during the first week on campus. This is not unusual, considering the freshman's quick shift from home to independence.

As you proceed with your interviews, *you may not enter any item more than once.* **Interview time 10 minutes!**

	Positives	Negatives
1.	_____	_____
2.	_____	_____
3.	_____	_____
4.	_____	_____
5.	_____	_____
6.	_____	_____
7.	_____	_____
8.	_____	_____
9.	_____	_____
10.	_____	_____

After the quick interviews the instructor should hold an open discussion, beginning by asking each student which feelings or experiences he or she had in common with the other students in the class. The most prevailing feelings within the group should be discussed, so that students can share coping strategies for the "negatives" and pursue the "positives" together.

Closure: This kind of activity, called an ice-breaker, is designed to encourage the sharing of feelings. The quick interviews give you an opportunity to speak face to face to ten people in your group, which breaks down the feeling of being alone.

Individual Exercise 1.4 *The Campus Inventory*

Purpose: Most college campuses have a variety of support services that can help you solve the common problems of student life. Many of these are explained in *College Is Only the Beginning* and *Step by Step to College Success* by Gardner and Jewler. If you are aware of these services, you can get help when you need it, thereby increasing your potential for survival and success as a student. If you have a problem and cannot locate the help you need, your quality of life and student performance will suffer until the problem is solved.

Directions: Below is a list of common support areas found on most campuses. Depending on the nature of your particular school, some of these areas will be emphasized more than others. Nevertheless, all are important. Your instructor will supply the name of your campus office in the space opposite each generic function. Find one of these offices, interview the person in charge to determine what services are provided, and obtain one pamphlet or handout for each member of the class. In Group Activity 1.5 you can share the information with each other.

Generic Functions	Your Campus Office
Study skills	_____
Drug and alcohol problems	_____
Anxiety and stress problems	_____
Assertiveness training	_____
Career planning/placement	_____
Religious counseling	_____
Commuter services	_____
Disabled student services	_____
Financial aid/scholarship	_____
Student entertainment programs	_____

Generic Functions	Your Campus Office
Housing services	_____
Intramural/recreational sports	_____
Legal services	_____
Library (services available)	_____
Health services	_____
Student employment	_____
Volunteer services	_____
Writing/tutorial center	_____
Greek affairs	_____
Student government	_____
Peer counseling programs	_____
Other	_____
Other	_____

Closure: At the conclusion of this exercise you should know at least one office with valuable student services. In Group Activity 1.5 you will have an opportunity to share the information that you have gathered.

Group Activity 1.5 *Campus Resources Presentation*

Purpose: This activity is designed to enable all students to share the resources they discovered in Exercise 1.4. In addition, each student will get some experience making a presentation with a handout. (A handout can serve as a good outline of what you will say in the presentation.)

Directions: Each student should be given three minutes to report what he or she learned on the visit to an office on campus.

Begin your presentation by giving each student in class a pamphlet or handout that describes the services at the office you visited. Allow the class to look over the handout before you begin speaking. If you don't, their attention will be divided between your presentation and the pamphlet. Be supportive of your classmates. Some will be better speakers than others, but everyone is there to learn.

Closure: Obviously, this activity works on several levels. Initially, you were sharing valuable information about your campus. On another level, you were practicing your communication skills. If you felt uncomfortable while giving your presentation, you were having a normal reaction to presenting to a group. You should consider taking a course in public speaking. Most students benefit from such courses, which are usually a lot of fun, very supportive, and a good way to learn skills you need for career success.

Trivia Teaser: "The ropes" refers to the ropes that control the sails on a ship. One who knew the ropes could sail the ship. One who did not know the ropes could easily get into trouble.

Journal Entry

You have just launched a great beginning. Many thoughts and feelings are whirling inside you. You have concerns for your ability to survive, to get along, to fit in, to be accepted, and more. If you are a resident, you are concerned about getting along with your roommate. If you are a commuter, you need the support (and patience) of your family because of the new demands college places on your life.

Gather yourself together. Buy a notebook or make one. Make it your personal writing space. Begin today. Write about the feelings you experience this first week of your college career. In years to come you may look back at this moment as a turning point or an awakening in your life.

❖ Chapter 2 ❖

College
Making a Difference in Your Life

In *College Is Only the Beginning*, Hilda F. Owens tells students that college prepares people "to develop a new flexibility, mobility, and knowledge needed to adapt to the changing demands of work and life." This flexibility has had a great impact on the way my friends and I approach the notion of career development. I have seen an electrical engineer become a world-renowned photographer, because he let his hobby go where it would, and a biologist turn into a developer of a unique carpentry service. As for me, I never dreamed of being a writer before computer spelling checkers arrived to balance my dyslexia. Nor could I have predicted my roles as an international consultant in executive foreign transfer or an organic vegetable and goat farmer in a quiet spot in Pennsylvania. I hope you will find, as many college graduates have, that higher education opens the world within you to meet the world outside.

The second point in Owens's essay is that college graduates find life to be more interesting. If you are intrigued by something, you enjoy it, you are motivated to do more of it, you need less sleep, you get ideas in your off hours and write them down, and you talk to others who share your interests. The result of following your interest is that you become the best in the field, make significant contributions, become recognized and successful. The first step is to build interests.

The Map = Your Interests

Interest has to be based on your already existing personality. Your education becomes an extension of your foundation if you approach it with the willingness to try something new just to see whether it's fun. Our society gives students the right to explore. Take advantage of this right and give yourself permission to develop your educational game plan from your interests, rather than from some requirements imposed by an institution. You will never regret it.

In the exercise that follows, I want you to conduct your own guided survey or evaluation of the academic courses that are offered at your college with only one criterion in mind: How do the courses offered line up with your interests; that is, how much use and fun will they be for you?

Individual Exercise 2.1 *Developing Your Interests*

Purpose: I have heard a lot of reasons for taking courses: To get the requirement out of the way. Because I need it for my major. It's a prerequisite. I need one more social science distribution. My adviser said I would like it. My roommate liked this course. And the list goes on. The best reason to take a course is that it gives you a tour of something you find interesting. I had always wondered what life was like in prehistoric times and had read some on the subject before college. I took 18 credits of history in college to discover how civilization grew out of the prehistoric tribal arrangement I had read about. I felt like a lucky kid going to story hour while everyone else had to attend class.

This two-part exercise will help you identify topics that you will find interesting. It may take a little time. But a stitch in time saves nine. (**Trivia Teaser:** What form of thinking is the previous statement, how does it work, and what is its origin? See the end of the chapter for the answer.)

Directions, Part 1: Chart 2.1A lists some common sources that can help you define your interest areas. Locate the site or common source. Look through the stories or topics that are located at that site or source, and note which ones interest you. Make a note of your interests in the space provided in the middle column. In the right column, list your previous experience, media exposure, or reading related to the topic. Be sure to transfer this list to Chapter 4 so that your adviser can help you find more courses that match your interests.

Interest Discovery Tours Itinerary 2.1A

Site	Topic of Interest	Your Previous Exposure
The textbook area of your college bookstore	1. ___ 2. ___ 3. ___	___ ___ ___
The non-textbook area of your college bookstore	1. ___ 2. ___ 3. ___	___ ___ ___
A magazine store	1. ___ 2. ___ 3. ___	___ ___ ___
The *New York Times*	1. ___ 2. ___ 3. ___	___ ___ ___
An encyclopedia	1. ___ 2. ___ 3. ___	___ ___ ___
Reader's Guide to Periodical Literature	1. ___ 2. ___ 3. ___	___ ___ ___

Directions, Part 2: Look over all the courses in your college catalog, keeping in mind the interests you have identified in Part 1,
plus others that might occur to you. Determine which five courses
look like they would be fun or interesting to you. *Fun or interest is
your only basis of judgment in this exercise.* In the space provided
below, write in the name and number of the course and the reason
the course appears as though it could be fun or interesting to you.
Your reasons may sound ridiculous to others. That's OK. They
don't have to take the course or live your life. List the most interesting or most fun in Number 1 and rank the courses. **Rule:** Four of
the five courses must be from different departments.

Suggestion: Enter your favorite courses in pencil and feel free to
change your selection at any time.

1. Most interesting or fun course title _____ no._____

    Why does this course appear to be interesting or fun for you? _____

    _____

    _____

2. Second most interesting or fun title _____ no._____

    Why does this course appear to be interesting or fun for you? _____

    _____

    _____

3. Third most interesting or fun title _____ no._____

    Why does this course appear to be interesting or fun for you? _____

    _____

    _____

4. Fourth most interesting or fun title _____ no._____

    Why does this course appear to be interesting or fun for you? _____

    _____

    _____

5. Fifth most interesting or fun title _____ no._____

   Why does this course appear to be interesting or fun for you?_____

   _____

   _____

Closure: This exercise was to help you design your education as a natural extension of your interests. This strategy is the surest ticket to college success: motivation from interest. Remember: The marketplace demands will change, your interests will remain and grow.

In Chapter 4 you will find an academic planning worksheet on page 38. Distribute your fun or interesting courses over the next two or three terms, making sure the most interesting is taken first. Pay attention to prerequisites and include them in your planning.

Group Activity 2.2 *Reasons for Having Fun*

Purpose: The best way to get new ideas is to ask others. During this activity you will share the results of your interest searches with the other members of your class. When you complete this activity you may find yourself wanting to change your list of five interesting or fun courses—why not? They're in pencil, aren't they?

Directions: Form groups of five students or less. Each group must determine: **(1)** the most popular courses as determined by the members of the group in the previous exercise; **(2)** as many different reasons as the group can think of for taking the course; **(3)** the five most unusual courses identified by members of the group.

After the groups have made their choices, a recorder from each group should write the group's selections on the board and call on members of their group to explain their interest in the course. The class at large should also contribute reasons for taking each course. List all reasons on the board or a flip chart under each course.

Each student should select at least one course and record all the reasons for taking the course(s) that the class could discover. Next, the student should produce a legible copy of the course title and number and the reasons, submit this to the professor who teaches that course, and ask: **(1)** Are these valid reasons for taking this course? **(2)** Are there other reasons for taking this course that have not been discovered by the class? Within two weeks of the beginning of this exercise, each student should be prepared to report to the class on the feedback from the professor.

Each student should make a brief report to the class, using a flip chart page, poster, or chalkboard to indicate the addition or deletion of reasons for taking the selected course, according to the recommendations of the interviewed professor.

Closure: This activity should have given you a new perspective on why you might like to select some courses that are offered at your college. Many students who follow this method of choosing courses change their majors to fields that are more fun and exciting for them.

Defining and Determining Life Needs

The purpose of this section is to get you to try on a different set of lenses as you look over your college's academic offerings. Try to think of the many roles that you will play in your life. The roles should include your personal life—perhaps a parent, or an explorer who knows several languages and can read maps. Roles not directly associated with career roles, such as doctors or accountants being bad-news deliverers, are often overlooked in academic planning. Of all the courses I have ever taken, I have to rank personal typing among the most important at this moment. I can tell you that a good parent must learn everything from how to be a good friend to understanding the emotional, psychological, and nutritional needs of growing children. Give some thought to your own possible life roles before entering the developmental exercise below.

Individual Exercise 2.3 *Defining Roles and Needs*

Purpose: The purpose of this exercise is to help you clarify your vision of what some of your social roles will be in your life. Your ability to act out the roles required of a successful person in our society will greatly increase your possibilities for success and reduce your level of anxiety and frustration.

Directions, Part 1: The first section of this exercise is designed to give you an idea of some of the basic roles successful people play in this society. Next to the role in the chart that follows is a generic listing of the content you might look for in a college course to better prepare you for the role. This is only a hint of the possible roles that you might play, not an exhaustive list. Add your own to the last category and continue with the exercise.

Success Roles in America

Roles	Generic Content
Parent	nutrition info, child psychology, education
Wage earner	bookkeeping, tax paying
Home owner	plumbing, gardening, repairing, shopping
Business person	networking, communication
Professional	expert in one field, knowledge of related fields
Other	_____
Other	_____

The chart was offered to give you a general idea of some roles you might play and the knowledge and skills you will have to acquire to perform the roles well. The purpose of the next part of the exercise is help you proceed logically from *roles* to *knowledge or skill* needed to perform well to *a course* that might help you acquire the knowledge or skill.

Directions: In the space provided, state some of the roles you think you might have to, or want to, take on in your life. Fill in the information that follows as best you can.

1. Expected role: _____

   What knowledge you need to play this role: _____

   _____

   _____

   What skills you need to play this role: _____

   _____

   _____

Courses that will enhance needed knowledge: _____

_____

_____

Courses that will enhance needed skills: _____

_____

_____

What extracurricular or outside activities would help you prepare for this role?

_____

_____

2. Expected role: _____

What knowledge you need to play this role: _____

_____

_____

What skills you need to play this role: _____

_____

_____

Courses that will enhance needed knowledge: _____

_____

_____

Courses that will enhance needed skills: _____

_____

_____

What extracurricular or outside activities would help you prepare for this role?

_____

_____

3. Expected role: _____

What knowledge you need to play this role: _____

_____

_____

What skills you need to play this role: _____

_____

Courses that will enhance needed knowledge: _____

_____

_____

Courses that will enhance needed skills: _____

_____

_____

What extracurricular or outside activities would help you prepare for this role?

_____

_____

Group Activity 2.4 *Relating Roles to Courses*

Purpose: Just as in Group Activity 2.2, in which your classmates shared with you what they discovered about interesting or fun courses, this activity will help you expand your awareness of life roles and the knowledge and skills needed to perform them well.

Directions: Sit in a circle and elect a recorder. Using a flip chart (taping the pages around the room) or a large chalkboard, the recorder will post all your expected roles as you go around the circle, each taking a turn reading his or her roles from Exercise 2.3.

The recorder should write the roles so that everyone can see them, leaving plenty of space under each one.

After all roles are posted, the recorder should direct the class to brainstorm about all the possible things you should know in order to be successful in the role in question.

Finally, the class should nominate courses or activities that would best prepare you to be successful in each role.

Individual Exercise 2.5 *How Will College Change Your Life?*

Purpose: This exercise is designed to show you the best way to get the graduates' view on how college can change your life: Ask them. Their viewpoint is valuable to obtain because it will give you a much better idea of what to look for when making your course selection. If you involve yourself in this exercise, you will get some appreciation for what we mean when we say that a college education can make life more interesting.

Directions: Select two people over the age of 35 who have a college degree. They should be successful in whatever sense you care to define the term. They should be happy with their work as far as you can tell. Contact each person. Explain that you have an interview assignment for your class and ask whether you can have a few minutes of his or her time to ask some questions about his or her college experience and how it affected his or her life. Interviews are always better when conducted in person, but if that is not possible, a telephone interview will do.

Ask the following questions. Sometimes a tape recorder can be useful if you are not used to taking fast notes. Be sure to ask permission before recording.

- ❖ Where did you go to college?
- ❖ Why did you go to college?
- ❖ What was your major in college and how does it relate to your career?
- ❖ What did you learn in college that has been useful in your career/private life?
- ❖ What skills did you learn in college that have been useful in your career/private life?
- ❖ If you compare your life experience to that of non–college graduates, how would you describe the difference college has made in your life?

❖ What advice can you give me as a freshman in college?

Requirement: Within 24 hours after the interview, send a short note (neatly typed or written) to both interviewees thanking them for their time and insights. Give a copy to your instructor.

Closure: This exercise should have given you a fairly clear picture of how some graduates value their college experience. In addition to the content of the information you obtained in the interview, you should have also gained some insight into interviewing skills. If you felt uneasy or reluctant to pursue this activity to the fullest, you might consider a discussion course to help you develop interviewing skills.

Group Activity 2.6 *Debriefing the Interview*

Purpose: Some of you will stumble into great interviews, whereas others might expect a lot and get almost nothing. With the short, but valuable, debriefing process that follows, you will be able to share the best of the interview experiences.

Directions: Form small groups of no more than five students. Summarize the highlights of the interviews within the group. Each group should appoint a spokesperson to relate the group discussion to the others in the class, paying particular attention to the advice obtained and the difference college made in people's lives.

Closure: In addition to the insights from discussions about the interviews, you might have gotten a glimpse into the values and decision-making process of your peers. What others say may sound great; however, if it is not right for you, stick to your own feelings and decisions on the matter. Every student has to design his or her own schedule, because in many ways the course schedule becomes the design for your life.

Group Activity 2.7 *The Campus Map*

Purpose: You have been on campus for a little while now. Yet you still know very little about the physical plant of your college. This activity is a good way to have some fun in class, while getting some feedback on your knowledge of the campus. During the process you will also find out some new and valuable information about your campus.

Directions: All students should face a large chalkboard or piece of paper on the wall. The class should appoint two students to be "pencils." Pencil A is assigned to the left side of the chalkboard, pencil B to the right.

Pencils are allowed to write only what they are told to write by the other members of the class. Pencils are allowed to write only on their side of the chalkboard. While remaining in their seats, members of the class must direct the pencils to draw a map of the college campus that indicates buildings and the activities that go on in them.

Closure: You probably found out the location of some place that you have heard of in the past week. If so, you gained a valuable piece of information. Did you also learn that you have to be very exact in giving directions if you want someone else to do something your way? Ask the pencils which directions were helpful and which were confusing. If you learn to give clear directions, you may become a good manager or team leader some day.

Trivia Teaser: The form of thinking is proverbial (as compared to the inductive/deductive thinking that dominates our mind). A proverb is an ancient form of thought, often considered to be folk-lore: the wisdom of the folk. Proverbs are abstract maps of situations with an attitude attached (a stitch in time; an ounce of prevention). State a proverb, define the attitude it communicates, and explain how the attitude guides you in a situation. It is difficult to think of proverbs when asked for a list of them. They arise, or are recalled in the proverbial thinker's mind, when the particular situation occurs that fits the proverb. In primitive (first people) tribes, councils of elders make decisions by recalling all the proverbs that fit the situation under discussion. When they agree on the attitude that is most appropriate, the direction to be taken is announced to the tribe.

Journal Entry

Respond to the following questions in your journal: In what way did the exercises in this chapter help you clarify some of the advantages that college can add to your life experience? What situations produced the most positive and negative emotional reactions in you this week—what was the reaction and why do you think you had it?

❖ Chapter 3 ❖

Higher Education History and You

More than 2,000 years ago the tradition of higher education was born. In ancient times this tradition was called *artes liberales,* arts befitting a freeman. A direct relationship exists between the development of the liberal arts education that we have today and the development of democracy. The survival and prosperity of a free, democratic state depends on the ability of the citizens to think for themselves. Through the past 2,000 years the liberal arts were the mode of instruction for the ruling class. The citizens in ancient Greece, the medieval kings and queens of Europe, and the modern citizens of the United States of America all share in this education tradition.

Through the long history of the liberal arts education, the facilities—both buildings and books—and the social customs of selecting, teaching, and welcoming freshmen have evolved. Our orientation rituals and the right of access to education of minorities and women reflect the beliefs and values of our society. Today in the United States we hold that *all* people have the right to actively participate in a liberal arts education so that they can make their own decisions. That is why we have man-

datory primary and secondary education and the most extensive higher education system in the world.

While a professional education can teach you to perform
specialized tasks or functions (accounting, chemical analysis,
preparing medicinal compounds), a liberal arts education can
prepare you to become a decision maker. Most of the corpo-
rate leaders of today have educations that combined the liberal
arts with some courses in business. They have the skills of the
trade and the ability to make decisions about how to employ the
skills of the trade.

The purpose of this chapter is to help you recognize and
understand how a liberal arts education can prepare you to be
a decision maker in our democracy. Once you identify this aspect of higher education, you will be able to seek it out and acquire it in a systematic way. In a very practical sense, as you
build your schedule of courses, you will be able to plan the
proper balance to help you develop sound thinking and decision-making abilities.

Individual Exercise 3.1 *Recognizing the Liberal Arts in Great People*

Purpose: Much of your education has given you the details of the
accomplishments of rulers, leaders, thinkers, inventors, innova-
tors, and so on. The story of their accomplishments, perhaps with
the exception of Abraham Lincoln and a few others, ignores their
education and concentrates on their contributions. You might look
at the accomplishments of Jonas Salk, Eleanor Roosevelt, or Mar-
tin Luther King, Jr., and wonder in disbelief how you could ever
have such an impact on your society. The first thing you should
look at is how these people and other greats were prepared by
their education and their life experiences to make lasting contributions. Your chance to walk into history may come after you learn
the first step.

The purpose of this exercise is to help you examine the education of a great person so that you can see a liberal arts education at work.

Directions: Over the course of one week, ask as many people as possible to nominate one college-educated person who, in their eyes, has made a lasting contribution toward the improvement of the human condition—the betterment of life for all. Be sure to ask why they believe the contribution is worthwhile.

Select one of those nominated or your own choice and proceed to investigate his or her education. You would probably do well to review the person's biography or history for the details of early life experiences and education. Ask your professors what they might know about the relationship between the education and contribution of the person. As you proceed in your investigation, try to answer the questions below.

Education of a Great Person

Name of the person _____

Contribution of the person _____

Education level of the person's parents _____

1. How did this person approach his or her education? Why did he or she take that particular course of study? Were all courses required? Was there more than one system of education? Did he or she have a choice?

   _____

   _____

   _____

2. Would you define this person's education as a liberal arts education? Did he or she study history, philosophy, literature, science, mathematics, languages, and so on?

   _____

   _____

   _____

3. Did this person write or speak well? What influence do you think his/her education had on his/her basic skills?

_____

_____

_____

4. Do you see any relationship between what this person studied or where he/she studied and the contribution he/she made in life?

_____

_____

_____

5. What ideas did you find to be most interesting in this person's life or work? What courses could you take to help you to begin to understand this person's ideas or life's work?

_____

_____

_____

6. What problem did this person address in his/her work?

_____

_____

_____

7. What courses in your college or university address the same problem?

_____

_____

_____

Closure: By examining the education of a great person—one who has made a contribution to the improvement of the human condition—you can begin to acquire a healthy perspective on the role of education in your development. Too many students avoid courses because they believe they will not excel and get good grades in them. This kind of avoidance will prevent you from exploring the breadth and depth of the liberal arts. Try to find a great person who did not have a broad education in the liberal arts tradition. Whether formally instructed or self-taught, a person's way to such contribution and recognition is through understanding how to put ideas together in new ways. The best way to start is to learn all the existing ideas!

Group Activity 3.2 *Comparing Your Findings*

Purpose: Perspective is acquired from seeing and appreciating many points of view. In Exercise 3.1 you had the opportunity to view a liberal arts education in the life of one great person. By listening to each other's findings, you will be able to see trends in the life experience and education of the great contributors. You may begin to see that the paths to greatness often began with interests born from life experiences, grew and expanded in education, and culminated in fulfilling and creative careers.

Directions: Find a piece of paper about five feet long (five or six sections of untorn computer paper work well). Draw a line along the length of the paper representing the life of the person you investigated. Divide the line into the time spans that were meaningful in that person's life. You might note year of birth, age at the start of his or her education (whether at home or in school), age at graduation, age when contributions were made. Along the line, list the significant events or educational experiences in the person's life. Also list the subjects or areas that this individual studied. Make sure that you write large enough so that it can be read from 15 feet away.

Each class member posts his or her person's lifeline and experiences on the board and is allotted two minutes to point out the significant ages and events. Try to get all the lifeline posters up for everyone to see during one session. Conclude the session with a discussion on any trends indicated in the life experiences and educations of the great contributors.

Closure: By combining insights with classmates, you may develop a good understanding of how a liberal arts education can affect your life. Note any trends that you see and consider them when you talk with your adviser about course selection.

Group Activity 3.3 *The News About Your College or University*

Purpose: Most students don't know the mission, goals, and objectives of their college or university. While you are probably attending your school because of a program it offers, its convenient location, or personal economic factors, you probably do not know the mission or purpose for which your institution was founded. The programs and courses offered by a college or university should be direct outgrowths of its stated mission, goals, and objectives. How closely do the stated mission, goals, and objectives of your school resemble your personal values, goals, and objectives? This activity is designed to help you develop a clear conception of the purpose of your college or university so that you can compare it to your own educational purpose.

Directions: Form small groups containing three to five students. Each group is a newspaper staff. Decide within your group who will be the reporters: those who research and write versions of the story, and who will be the editor: the one who coordinates the efforts of reporters and directs the writing of the final story.

You are to write a news story of no more than two typed pages, double-spaced, with one-inch margins. Your topic is the founding of your college or university. You should be able to mention something about the mission, goals, and objectives of the institution as they are reflected in the courses and programs it offers.

Remember: All good news stories lead off with *who, what, why, when, where, and how.* You might want to read a respected newspaper like the *New York Times* or the *Christian Science Monitor* for some good examples of news stories. Circulate the stories around your class, revise them, submit a copy to your campus newspaper and/or post them on bulletin boards around campus.

Closure: The philosophy that guides your college or university will influence your college life. It is to your benefit to understand where your educators hope to lead you so that you can decide if you want to go in that direction.

Individual Exercise 3.4 *Summarizing Your Life*

Purpose: One of the best ways to plan the impact of your education on your life is to imagine your life on your last day. Define for yourself the course you would like your life to have followed.

Directions: Think about your own lifeline as you were asked to draw and explain the lifeline of great people in Exercise 3.1. When you reach the conclusion of your lifeline, write your obituary. Include your education and its relationship to the influence your life had on others or on society in general. Consult your local newspaper to see how obituaries are written. Limit yourself to 250 words.

Closure: There is something about facing the mortal limitations of our lives that helps us put things in perspective. What you learn in the next few years will influence, if not define, the rest of your life. If you learn to learn, you will spend your time learning and exploring whatever interests you.

Journal Entry

Which three liberal arts courses do you feel are most important and why?

❖ Chapter 4 ❖

Working with Your Adviser

The best advice is to never be satisfied with one person's advice. Seek many advisers, consider the bias of the adviser, and be sure that you seek those who are capable of giving good advice. Taking the advice of a roommate in academic and life-planning matters can be the blind leading the blind. Think about the general type that you are as you read the section that follows. This may be the first indication to you that the advice given to another may not be appropriate for you.

General Types/General Advice

The First-Generation College Student

If your parents did not go to college, they may not fully understand the nature of college education. They may never understand the difference between liberal arts and professional education. To many parents, post-secondary education may simply represent job opportunity. That is OK. In most cases parents mean well and want to do the best for their children. If you feel that their advice conflicts with that of your academic adviser, ask your parents whether they would like to discuss the situation with your adviser. I have had many conferences with parents, in my office and on the phone, usually improving the parents' understanding of higher education. Of course, an adviser should have the permission of the student before contacting the parents.

Chip Off the Old Block

It is not uncommon to listen to students and hear the parents talking. "Dad does 'x' and it looks like fun" . . . "my folks think I should" . . . "Mom and I are a lot alike and she . . ." Sometimes children do follow in the footsteps of their parents and are quite happy. I don't have a problem with that. But a career and a life are two different things. You can enter your parents' field, but you cannot live their life, or the life they wish they had led. Study what excites you. If you end up where your parents would like— fine. If not, they will probably be happy if you are happy and successful in your life and career. Sometimes they just can't imagine what you could become. And if they are caring parents, they are compelled to advise you from their experiences.

"I'd Like to Get This Out of the Way"

I'll bet I've heard that line a million times. Don't treat your requirements like hurdles or obstacles. It took a lot of educated and experienced people years of discussion to determine the structure of your school's requirements—most of which are fairly standard. Ask your adviser what value the requirement has for you; ask until you clearly understand. Make sure that you get the value into yourself so that you can take it with you at graduation. In the outside world the content in your mind is worth more than grades.

The Dollar Chaser

Making money and being successful are not always the same thing. Being successful is doing the work that you love to do, getting paid for it, and having the private life that suits your individual personality. Do what you like to do. You will be the best at what you do and you will rise to the top of the salary level in your field. Go after money and you will be mediocre in the field simply because the problems you must solve will not fascinate you as they do others.

The Working Student

There is nothing magical about four years. When you go to the store to buy groceries, do you just stuff any fruits and vegetables into your basket regardless of the quality, just to get out of the store on time? Would you take six eggs and pay for a dozen? If you work 20 hours a week and take a full course load, you may be doing just that. If you do not give yourself the time to learn all you can from a course, you are paying for the whole thing and taking half. Talk to your adviser about time management and alternative financing.

Individual Exercise 4.1 *Attitudes and Behaviors*

Purpose: The one thing few students learn is *how to be a student.* Most of what you do as a student is learned by trial and error. In high school, weak learning strategies are usually not fatal to the student. In college, only the best succeed. Step back for a moment and take a critical view of yourself as a student. Fear not! Weak or unsuccessful strategies can be changed fairly easily by distinguishing the successful from the unsuccessful. Then you simply opt to do one and not the other.

Directions: What follows are student strategies divided into two lists of attitudes and behaviors: those of successful and those of unsuccessful freshmen.[1] Review the lists, placing check marks in front of the behaviors that are similar to yours. You will be able to determine whether you are on a successful path or not. Try it now, and again in a few weeks. Be honest with yourself. Then be honest with your adviser. If you find that your total checks are higher in the unsuccessful column, tell your adviser. Good advice and some learning skills counseling can turn a losing trend into a success.

Successful Freshmen	Unsuccessful Freshmen
Prior attitudes	
❏ have sense of direction and expect to do things right	❏ anticipate better performance with change in environment
❏ have resolution to achieve certain academic goals	❏ think college = chance to undo past failures; "things will turn around"
❏ have examined and understood high school behavior	❏ think college will offer motivation
❏ think college = resources to be used and opportunity to realize goals	

---

[1]Adapted from Jack T. Ling, Ph.D., Boston University, "Profiles of Academically Strong and Weak Students at Boston University's College of Basic Studies: A Phenomenologically Oriented Pilot Study" (Draft of paper presented at the Fifth International Human Sciences Research Conference, Berkeley, Calif.)

	Successful Freshmen		Unsuccessful Freshmen

Successful Freshmen

- ❏ are ready to learn interesting things
- ❏ accept responsibility to make college meaningful

Classes start

Successful Freshmen

- ❏ experience anxiety mixed with hope and excitement
- ❏ look for people and ways to help them change
- ❏ intend to devote much free time to study

- ❏ consider quizzes and exams to be tests of efficacy of new strategy and approaches to learning
- ❏ when new strategies bring success, incorporate them as standard preparation for tests

- ❏ consider school a place to spend time, get involved
- ❏ seek help when results are not as expected; find more effective ways for particular subject
- ❏ talk with professors, staff, and other successful students
- ❏ feel school is a friendly place where people push and challenge you
- ❏ find a home
- ❏ motivated by drop in grades to work harder and to seek help

- ❏ take responsibility for failure and success
- ❏ in control of much of his/her college experience

- ❏ speak clearly about changes in college and how they occurred

Unsuccessful Freshmen

- ❏ experience discomfort and increasing anxiety
- ❏ respond to work demand with procrastination and avoidance
- ❏ use familiar high school strategy to get by—and fail
- ❏ in spite of failure, stay with old strategy

- ❏ have more work assigned "unexpectedly"

- ❏ find school becoming a place where things happen too soon or too late
- ❏ find academic demands to be uninteresting obligations; school activities become boring and meaningless
- ❏ avoid demanding teachers and difficult subjects
- ❏ feel school is unfriendly

- ❏ feel excluded
- ❏ study to avoid failure; old patterns remain: procrastination, wishful thinking, anxiety, guilt, last-minute frantic studying
- ❏ use repetition instead of planning
- ❏ notice particular shift in study habits gets results; feel relief—cause and effect not recognized; success is attributed to special circumstances
- ❏ find success is sporadic, infrequent, and unpredictable

Successful Freshmen	Unsuccessful Freshmen
❑ familiar with thinking about thinking	❑ seek outside help for specific pressing problems; sustained help seldom occurs
❑ have tremendous loyalty and attachment to college and particular professors	
	❑ if help is obtained and results are negative, others are blamed and support services are avoided
	❑ spurts of "hitting the books" are crowded by greater and growing involvement with distracting activities such as outside work, socializing, and complaining

Total checks _____   **Total checks** _____

Closure: Self-honesty is perhaps the most valuable and most difficult thing to achieve in life. We typically deny or ignore things that may cause us some discomfort. To be honest with yourself, you must first become aware of yourself. This exercise was one step toward self-knowledge. Be sure it is also a step in the right direction. If your checks are concentrated on the unsuccessful side, tell your adviser as soon as possible. Review the lists at the end of each term to evaluate your progress.

Individual Exercise 4.2 *Concluding Statement*

Purpose: Just looking at the list of attitudes and behaviors, recognizing your behaviors on the list, and moving on is not going to help you. To ensure the best possible results on the road to self-knowledge and self-improvement, you should make a step-by-step examination of your student style. The purpose of this exercise is to get you to react to each statement.

Directions: Based on your self-observations in Exercise 4.1, write a three-page statement *detailing* your successful or unsuccessful attitudes and behaviors, saying "I do this and I don't do that." Send copies to your adviser and to your freshman seminar instructor.

Closure: When this process is done well, it will take you beyond denying and ignoring aspects of yourself that could cause you some difficulty. Again, self-knowledge is not easy to obtain. However, the more self-knowledge you have, the more control you will have over the course of your life and the events around you.

Individual Exercise 4.3 *Your Academic Planning Sheet*

Purpose: The purpose of this exercise is to organize the results of your various course identification or course selection exercises. Most of the blanks should have already been filled in from your work in the first three chapters.

Directions: In the spaces provided, write in the information that you have developed in the exercises in the preceding chapters. Include requirements of your proposed major and requirements of your school or college.

Attention minority and international students: Refer to Chapter 15 to include the special considerations your situation or development requires before proceeding with your academic plan.

Academic Planning Sheet

Basic Skills Courses If Needed

Public speaking: _____

Computer science: _____

Study skills:_____

Five Fun or Interesting Courses

1._____

2._____

3._____

4._____

5._____

Courses on Problems

Problem:_____

_____

Courses:

1._____

2._____

3._____

4._____

5._____

Problem: _____

_____

Writing: _____

Math: _____

Reading: _____

Other:_____

Expected Life Role/Courses

1._____

Skill needed:_____

Skill course:_____

Knowledge needed: _____

_____

Knowledge course:_____

2._____

Skill needed: _____

Skill course: _____

Knowledge needed: _____

_____

Knowledge course: _____

3._____

Skill needed: _____

Skill course: _____

Knowledge needed: _____

_____

Courses: Knowledge course: _____

1. _____   _____

2. _____

3. _____   **College Requirements:**

4. _____   1. _____

5. _____   2. _____

                                           3. _____

Major Exploration Courses   4. _____
(*for shopping around*)
                                           5. _____

1.   _____   6. _____

2.   _____   7. _____

3.   _____   8. _____

4.   _____   9. _____

5.   _____   10. _____

Closure: This exercise should have given you a clearer idea of various interests that you might want to include in your academic plan in the next exercise.

Individual Exercise 4.4 *Undergraduate Academic Plan*

Purpose: Too often students make out their schedule only by considering what is offered next term and what requirements they want to get out of the way. I strongly urge you to look at the entire process. Imagine what you will take in your senior year and why. In this way you will see how education builds new knowledge and skills on acquired knowledge and skills.

Directions: *In pencil*, enter all the courses that you have identified as part of your educational program. Then show it to your ad-

viser and professionals in a field of interest to you for feedback.
Note that there are six years' worth of terms in the academic plan
for those students who are not going to graduate in four years.

First Term

1. _____

2. _____

3. _____

4. _____

5. _____

6. _____

Second Term

1. _____

2. _____

3. _____

4. _____

5. _____

6. _____

Third Term

1. _____

2. _____

3. _____

4. _____

5. _____

6. _____

Fourth Term

1. _____

2. _____

3. _____

4. _____

5. _____

6. _____

Fifth Term

1. _____

2. _____

3. _____

4. _____

5. _____

6. _____

Sixth Term

1. _____

2. _____

3. _____

4. _____

5. _____

6. _____

Seventh Term

1. _____

2. _____

3. _____

4. _____

5. _____

6. _____

Eighth Term

1. _____

2. _____

3. _____

4. _____

5. _____

6. _____

Ninth Term

1. _____

2. _____

3. _____

4. _____

5. _____

6. _____

Tenth Term	Eleventh Term	Twelfth Term
1._____	1._____	1._____
2._____	2._____	2._____
3._____	3._____	3._____
4._____	4._____	4._____
5._____	5._____	5._____
6._____	6._____	6._____

Closure: Seeing your entire education planned out is beneficial. You should be able to perceive a logic in it and be excited about it. If you don't see the logic, or feel the excitement, talk with your adviser.

Group Activity 4.5 *Comparing Plans*

Purpose: There is a time for individual advice and decisions as well as a time for sharing the overall picture with others. Hearing how your peers come to grips with some of the same problems you are working out can be helpful. This activity will give you the opportunity to compare your overall educational plans.

Directions: While seated in a circle, several students who have completed Exercises 4.3 and 4.4 should explain their academic plans and how they arrived at them. Those who have not completed Exercises 4.3 and 4.4 should explain where they are in the process, problems they are having, and when they will complete their plans and report to the group.

Closure: Hearing others talking about their academic plans probably gave you some new ideas. Look at your own plan and see how you can improve on your first draft.

Group Activity 4.6 *The Advising Process*

Purpose: Academic advising is a process that must be learned by both the adviser and the student. Most advisers go through a training period that informs them of college programs and majors, as well as ways of communicating with freshmen. The purpose of this activity is to help freshmen better understand the advising process, and to give advisers feedback on their style and questions.

Directions: Delegate two members of the group to invite their academic advisers to class. The advisers should role-play the advising situation with several students while the rest observe the process. After the role-play, the group and the advisers should discuss the following questions:

1. Was the student prepared to be advised?
2. Did the adviser ask good questions?
3. Did the student ask good questions?
4. What other questions should have been asked?
5. What is the difference between advising and registration?

Closure: This activity should have improved your understanding process. I hope you noted the fact that the student has a responsibility to contribute information and questions. Being prepared for an advising session means: **(1)** you have considered your options and all feedback from family, friends, professors, and test results; **(2)** you have made some preliminary decisions; and **(3)** you are ready to present them to your adviser for more questions and suggestions.

Journal Entry

Discuss your academic plan as a starting point for the rest of your life.

❖ Chapter 5 ❖

Study Skills

The average freshman has been a student for 12 years and has never had instruction on how to be a good student. Until very recent times, the assumption guiding our education system was that you learned to be a student by being a student. That is like saying that you can learn to become a good pilot by flying an airplane—perhaps true for those who survive the first flight and landing. To extend the metaphor: Too often, bailing out (dropping out or avoiding "hard" subjects) has been the common survival strategy. However, there are many things one can do before avoiding a class becomes the best alternative.

Most colleges and universities have a place and staff who help students with their study skills. There, you are likely to find courses or workshops in time management, test taking, note taking and review, reading comprehension in textbooks, novels, short stories, articles, and much more. For example, advice on learning how to read a textbook includes such tips as:

1. Review the assigned section, especially the questions at the end.
2. Identify the new terms and locate their definitions.

3. Review the chapter headings to get a sense of the overall outline or direction of the text.
4. Determine the conclusions reached in the selection so that you can follow the logic of it when you begin reading.
5. Read the selection.

First Survival, Then Success

As a freshman you are entering a new system. You may occasionally find yourself in a course that does not seem right for you. Think of study skills as academic success strategies and bailing out as a survival strategy. Employ the guidelines in the following exercise to help you determine a successful course of action.

Individual Exercise 5.1 *Basic Study Skills Evaluation*

Purpose: You may have some idea of how well your high school prepared you for the rigors of college. However, because problems with study skills rarely show up until the first term is a third or half over, the best success strategy is to evaluate your study skills early. If you have a weak area, you can work to strengthen it before you get into trouble. This exercise will supply you with the feedback you need to identify weaknesses and strengths in your study skills. This is also an exercise in self-knowledge—be honest with yourself!

Directions: Answer the questions on the answer form that follows the questions. On the answer form R = rarely, S = sometimes, F = frequently, and A = almost always. This test will help you determine the strength or weakness of your basic study skills. If you score low in any area ask your instructor or adviser to help you improve these critical skills.

Survey of Study Skills[1]

Textbook Reading

1. Do you read the introduction, headings, and subtitles of a chapter before you read the chapter?
2. When you read a chapter for the first time, is your primary intention to complete the reading and to attempt to learn it at some later time?
3. As you read, do you stop periodically to explain what you have read in your own words?
4. Is your motivation to begin a reading assignment negatively affected when you discover how many pages there are to read?
5. Do you read a portion of the material (several paragraphs) before you attempt to underline or take notes on the important information?
6. Do you attempt to complete an entire chapter in one long study session?
7. Do you pay attention to graphs, charts, or diagrams contained in reading material?
8. Do you find that you must reread a passage because you have been reading words instead of the ideas?
9. Do you attempt to analyze how ideas are organized and related to each other?
10. Do you have difficulty selecting the important information from an assigned reading?

Lecture Notes

11. Do you familiarize yourself with assigned readings before the material is presented in lecture?
12. Do you miss important information because your mind is on something other than what the lecturer is saying?
13. Do you leave a wide margin or a side of the page blank to provide for reorganizing or adding ideas to your notes after the lecture?
14. Do you have difficulty determining what information you should include in your lecture notes?
15. Do you indent your notes so that you can visually determine different levels of importance?
16. When you review your notes, do you have difficulty explaining what they mean in your words?
17. Do you reorganize (not necessarily rewrite) your notes so that

[1]*Source:* Georgine Materniak, "Study Skills Survey," University of Pittsburgh Learning Skills Center. Reprinted by permission.

they reflect your understanding of the material?

18. Do you perform your first major review of lecture material just before an exam?
19. Do you attempt to relate lecture and textbook information?
20. Do you have difficulty accurately predicting what lecture information will be included in your exams?

Memory

21. Do you attempt to cluster and categorize information that you want to remember?
22. Do you rely primarily on repetition or memorization as devices for remembering information?
23. Do you try to explain material in your own words?
24. Do you attempt to remember everything without making a conscious decision as to why it should be remembered?
25. Do you review text and lecture information on at least a weekly basis?
26. Do you find that you depend on all-night reviews to remember information for an exam?
27. Do you draw pictures, charts, diagrams, and so on as methods of remembering material?
28. Do you study for long periods of time without taking a break?
29. Do you develop an organized plan as to how you will attempt to remember information?
30. Do you find that you must spend a lot of time relearning something you thought you knew?

Study Attitudes and Organization

31. When you begin to study, do you know exactly what and how much you intend to learn?
32. Do you find yourself in a cycle of worrying about what you are not accomplishing, which makes it more difficult to get anything accomplished?
33. Is your main purpose for studying to learn rather than to just get it done?
34. Do you have difficulty meeting deadlines or completing assignments because of procrastination?
35. After the first few weeks of a new term, do you develop a consistent routine of studying particular subjects on certain days of the week?
36. Do daydreams or distractions keep you from accomplishing your study goals?
37. Do you refer to your course syllabus or outline as a guide for determining what you need to learn?

38. Are your study plans determined primarily by your moods or by what you feel like studying?
39. Do you feel that the amount of effort you put into studying is reflected in your grades?
40. Do you study in an environment that is likely to create interruptions, distractions, or noise?

Test Strategies

41. In preparing for an exam, do you create an organized plan as to what you need to learn and when you will review?
42. Do you quickly look through your notes and books as you are waiting for the exam to begin?
43. Do you try to predict questions that may be on the exam and rehearse the answers to those questions?
44. Do you find that memorization is the most important factor in preparing for an objective test?
45. When a test question is ambiguous, do you ask the instructor for clarification?
46. Do you have difficulty discriminating between partially correct and correct choices on a multiple choice test?
47. Do you organize your ideas before you begin to write an essay answer?
48. Do you find that you recall answers to questions that you did not know just after you leave the exam room?
49. Do you remain unaffected by the fact that other students have completed the exam before you?
50. Do you make errors on exams because you have read questions inaccurately?

Score Sheet

Textbook Reading

R S F A	R S F A
1. 0 0 0 0	2. 0 0 0 0
3. 0 0 0 0	4. 0 0 0 0
5. 0 0 0 0	6. 0 0 0 0
7. 0 0 0 0	8. 0 0 0 0
9. 0 0 0 0	10. 0 0 0 0

Textbook Reading

Score: _____

Lecture Notes

R S F A	R S F A
11. 0 0 0 0	12. 0 0 0 0
13. 0 0 0 0	14. 0 0 0 0
15. 0 0 0 0	16. 0 0 0 0
17. 0 0 0 0	18. 0 0 0 0
19. 0 0 0 0	20. 0 0 0 0

Lecture Notes

Score:_____

Memory

R S F A	R S F A
21. 0 0 0 0	22. 0 0 0 0
23. 0 0 0 0	24. 0 0 0 0
25. 0 0 0 0	26. 0 0 0 0
27. 0 0 0 0	28. 0 0 0 0
29. 0 0 0 0	30. 0 0 0 0

Memory

Score:_____

Study Attitudes and Organization

	R S F A				R S F A		
31.	0 0 0 0			32.	0 0 0 0		
33.	0 0 0 0			34.	0 0 0 0		
35.	0 0 0 0			36.	0 0 0 0		
37.	0 0 0 0			38.	0 0 0 0	Attitudes/Organization	
39.	0 0 0 0			40.	0 0 0 0	Score:_____	

Test Strategies

	R S F A				R S F A		
41.	0 0 0 0			42.	0 0 0 0		
43.	0 0 0 0			44.	0 0 0 0		
45.	0 0 0 0			46.	0 0 0 0		
47.	0 0 0 0			48.	0 0 0 0	Test Strategies	
49.	0 0 0 0			50.	0 0 0 0	Score:_____	

Note: Scoring instructions are at the end of this chapter just before the Journal Entry. *Do not look at them until after* you have answered all of the questions.

Interpreting the Results of Your Study Skills Survey

Circle the range that includes your score for each of the five study skills categories on the graph below.

	Textbook Reading	Lecture Notes	Memory	Study Attitudes & Organization	Test Strategies
Excellent	30–26	30–26	30–26	30–26	30–26
Good	25–20	25–20	25–20	25–20	25–20
Average	19–15	19–15	19–15	19–15	19–15
Below average	14–0	14–0	14–0	14–0	14–0

What the Graph Means

The graph enables you to see at a glance which skills are strong and which skills you may need to improve. What do the ranges mean?

Excellent   You are currently using productive and efficient methods. You do not need to change what you are doing.

Good   You do not need to change what you are doing but may want to increase the efficiency of those methods.

Average   You need to make some changes in what you are doing, and you need to increase the efficiency of some of your methods.

Below average   You must make changes in that particular skill. If not, you will have difficulties that could be prevented by learning more effective and efficient methods.

Item Analysis

Now that you know your general profile, let's get more specific. You should now do an item analysis to determine specific techniques that you need to change.

For those items that had either a *zero* or a *one* score, circle the question number on your survey question form. These are the specific items that must be changed if you are to reach your full learning potential.

Individual Exercise 5.2 *Time Management Inventory*

Purpose: In high school your time was mostly planned for you. Study halls, class schedules, parental restrictions all had an influence on how you spent your time. Time management is a skill we all must learn if we are to succeed in our professions. If you learn to manage your time now, you will be able to include more in your college experience—and have more successes. This exercise is designed to help you learn this valuable skill.

Directions: Use Form 5.2A on pp. 53–54 to log your time use for the next week, beginning tomorrow when you wake. **Note:** Photocopy the forms before using them so that you can have them to use again. By now you should have established a pattern. Record your pattern here so that you can take an objective look at it. When your time use is recorded for one week, proceed to Exercise 5.3.

Individual Exercise 5.3 *Time Management: The Basic Skill*

Purpose: The purpose of this exercise is to show you how to define your high-energy time and your wasted time, so that you can use time more productively.

Directions: Follow the instructions to fill in your work and recreation schedule for next week. Use Form 5.2A to improve your use of time. **Note:** If you are employed, be sure to weigh the impact of your work hours on your learning time.

Answer the following:

1. How many hours of sleep do you need each night?   _____

2. How many hours of sleep averaged Monday to Friday last week?   _____

3. Subtract Line 2 from Line 1: Total hours needed sleep *lost per week* =   _____

4. How many hours are there between your classes?   _____

5. How many between-class hours do you need to work or eat?   _____

6. Subtract Line 5 from Line 4: *"Between hours" you could study* =   _____

Answer the following questions about the previous week. If you cannot answer yes, figure out why.

1. Did you get up early enough to eat breakfast before class?
2. Did you have some physical exercise/recreation each day?
3. If you had a favorite project to do and freedom to do it any time of day, when would you do it? These should be your high-energy hours—for most people they are early in the day. Did you use your high-energy hours for study and going to classes?
4. Did you spend about three hours studying for every one hour in class?
5. Did you restrict your socializing to the more relaxing hours of the evening to prepare yourself for a good night's sleep?
6. Were you prepared in advance for tests, quizzes, and papers so that you did not have to stay up all night to get your work finished?
7. Did you avoid partying during the week nights?

Time Organizer 5.2A

	Monday __/__	Tuesday __/__	Wednesday __/__	Thursday __/__	Friday __/__
7:00					
8:00					
9:00					
10:00					
11:00					
12:00					
1:00					
2:00					
3:00					
4:00					
5:00					
6:00					
7:00					
8:00					
9:00					
10:00					
11:00					
12:00					
1:00					
2:00					
3:00					
4:00					

Time Organizer 5.2A

	Saturday __/__	Sunday __/__
7:00		
8:00		
9:00		
10:00		
11:00		
12:00		
1:00		
2:00		
3:00		
4:00		
5:00		
6:00		
7:00		
8:00		
9:00		
10:00		
11:00		
12:00		
1:00		
2:00		
3:00		
4:00		

Your Week at a Glance

Exams & Quizzes

Subject	Date

Reading

Subj.	Book	Pages	Date due

Papers

Subject	Date

Special Study Sessions

Alone or group	Subject	Place	Date/time	Materials

Exercise & Recreation

Event	Date/time

Social Event

Event	Date/time

Review for Next Week

Making an Ideal Work and Recreation Schedule

Fill in the Time Organizer chart for next week so that you will be able to answer yes to the preceding questions and avoid any wasted time that you may have discovered in the first six questions.

Closure: At this point you should have filled in the time you should be: **(1)** in class, **(2)** at work, **(3)** studying, **(4)** relaxing. Be sure to use the week-at-a-glance section to help you organize and prepare for assignments and exams.

Group Activity 5.4 *Study Skills Awareness*

Purpose: The purpose of this section is to help you share your study skills knowledge and correct your study skills misconceptions.

Directions: Divide the class so that at least two students will be responsible for leading a class discussion on the following topics:

1. The difference between kinds of tests and how to study for each.
2. How to read an article, textbook, short story, poem, and novel
3. How to study for and take an essay exam
4. How to take, organize, and study notes
5. How to listen intelligently
6. How to get help when you need it

Tips for Running a Discussion

1. Know your subject completely: Read about it and interview experts.
2. Devise a set of questions that will draw on the experience of the larger group so that the experience of one may become a point of instruction for all.
3. Never make fun of or embarrass one of the group. Some people can talk about negative experiences, others cannot.
4. Ask your questions as a way of proceeding through your material. Add your information only to fill in the gaps or to summarize.
5. Act as the group leader and have assistants who are experts on specific fine points that the leader can call on for clarification.

Closure: In addition to sharing some valuable information on study skills, you should have learned more about running a discussion. In some ways the latter is the more valuable part of the activity. This kind of communication is common in business and other organizations.

Group Activity 5.5 *Time Management Feedback*

Purpose: One of the best ways to learn about a topic is to explore it in an essay. The act of writing for an audience should make you a little more conscious of your logic and a little more careful about your facts. This activity will help you refine your insights into study skills while making you more aware of the writing process.

Directions: Write a short essay (300 words) on comparing your old time management procedures with your new ones. Select from the class an editorial board of three students. The board must choose one essay to be sent to the school newspaper. The selection will be based on the following criterion: the essay's ability to inspire others to see the benefits of good time management and perhaps employ positive time management practices.

Closure: With so many writing on the same subject, discussions may have occurred that helped you refine your ideas. The concept of time management becomes more familiar with each usage. Also, in the process you were able to practice your writing.

Journal Entry

Discuss the impact of time management on your day. Do you spend a lot of time socializing? Do you feel that you have your time under control? Are you ready for midterm exams?

Scoring the Study Skills Survey

To score the survey, notice that all odd-numbered answers make up one column and that all even-numbered answers make up a second column. The *odd*-numbered questions are considered to be effective and efficient strategies for learning; *even*-numbered questions are considered to be ineffective and inefficient strategies. Therefore, the scoring system is most easily set up by assigning the values to the columns in the manner demonstrated below.

R=Rarely, S=Sometimes, F=Frequently, A=Always

	values:	0 1 2 3		values:	3 2 1 0
		R S F A			R S F A
Odd numbers:	1 to 49	0 0 0 0	Even numbers:	2 to 50	0 0 0 0

Using the scoring code at the top of the two columns, count up the total number of points for each of the five skills categories and enter each score in the appropriate score line.

Turn to the graph that follows the score sheet, circle your score range below each skill column, and begin to evaluate the results.

❖ Chapter 6 ❖

Decoding Your Professor

Decoding People: The First Stage in Communication

One view of communication is that it is a set of skills to be learned in composition and speech classes. That is the view of the uninformed. In reality, successful communicators spend a considerable amount of their professional lives writing letters, memos, proposals, reports, outlines, books, articles, and sometimes an occasional poem or short story. At other moments we find ourselves reporting at meetings, giving lectures, interviewing people, selling an idea, seeking information, making formal phone invitations, and so on.

These modes of writing and speaking are our formal systems of communication for successful enterprise. However, they are by no means the only ways we communicate. Another realm, which is often unconscious and yet conveys 90 percent of the message, is *nonverbal communication.*

Suppose I sent you an elegant hand-printed invitation to come to my home, followed it up with a personal phone call, and when you arrived at my house you found that I had just gone camping and the painters were clearing the furniture out of the living room? The written and spoken forms were all correct—but the nonverbal gave you another message. What if I said, "I'm glad to see you" while I put my hands in my pockets and walked away? What would the message be if a friend invited me to his church and in the middle of the ceremony I shouted out his name and yelled: "I hope I'm not embarrassing you, but I really respect this place!" Or if I came to your wedding with dirt all over my weekend clothes? In each case the nonverbal communication speaks louder than the formal forms of writing and speaking.

When we plan our communication with others, the nonverbal aspect must be taken into consideration. In many ways the *nonverbal is the context of the communication situation.* It is the container of the communication. The container should reflect the quality of the product inside. Do diamonds and jelly beans come in the same box?

In the following pages you will find interaction exercises designed to help you establish some of the physical, social, and academic communication patterns you need to become a successful student. The exercises will help you develop a healthy relationship with your faculty and peers. Such exercises should be done in a supportive nonverbal context: Don't have the stereo or TV blasting or people visiting while you are interviewing your professor. Instead, get yourselves in a comfortable, relaxed, open posture at a predetermined time and calmly proceed out of respect for yourselves and each other during the interview.

In a very pragmatic sense, people communicate to get

what they need. Getting your needs fulfilled should be your first objective as you proceed through these interactions. Define your needs early; redefine them as they change. Communicate your needs to those who directly affect your space and time.

Individual Exercise 6.1 *Identifying Successful Student Behaviors*

Purpose: The first step in molding your communication style into successful student behaviors is to recognize the behaviors that you want to take on and to determine exactly how they are performed. This exercise will help you to identify some successful behaviors.

Directions: In *College Is Only the Beginning* and *Step by Step to College Success*, Gardner and Jewler offer advice on how to make the most of your student-professor relationship and on what professors want from their students. Of their suggestions and observations (listed below), which are purely nonverbal and which are a combination of formal writing, speaking, and nonverbal?

Before each statement indicate whether the advice directs you in nonverbal communication (nc), written communication (wc), or spoken communication (sc), or perhaps nc-wc-sc.

_____   1.   Come to class regularly and be on time.
_____   2.   Come to class well groomed and properly dressed.
_____   3.   Read all the assigned material before class.
_____   4.   Ask questions frequently.
_____   5.   Show interest in the subject.
_____   6.   Sit near the front of the class.
_____   7.   Never talk or whisper while the professors are lecturing.
_____   8.   Don't hand your professors a lot of "bull."
_____   9.   Participate in class discussion.
_____ 10.   Complete your assignments on time.
_____ 11.   Ask questions during class.
_____ 12.   Make appointments to see your professors.
_____ 13.   Comment on lecture materials.
_____ 14.   Simply smile and say "hello" when you meet on campus.
_____ 15.   Maintain frequent eye contact with professor during class.

_____ **16.** Share a story or anecdote.

_____ **17.** Joke with your professors or the class when appropriate.

_____ **18.** Show that you realize the value of what they're teaching you.

_____ **19.** Excuse yourself when you miss class for a legitimate reason such as illness (so that your professor realizes what you missed and that you care that you missed and want to make it up).

Closure: After reviewing the list and identifying the kinds of communication used in each behavior, you should have found several new strategies for communicating a positive attitude to your faculty. In pursuing this kind of communication in the classroom, you will also increase your attention power, retain more facts, and develop a better understanding of the theoretical level.

Gardner and Jewler distill the unspoken protocol of the classroom in Suggestions 1–18. I added Number 19. I develop an honest respect for the student who excuses him/herself for missing a class because of illness or some other legitimate reason. The student is indicating that he/she sees value in my teaching. At that moment of politeness and respect (best done at the end of class), I will make an effort to talk to the student to help him/her make up the missed material and to get to know him/her as a person.

Awareness of the nonverbal factors and classroom protocols can help you succeed as a student, and practice in the skills of communication will prove to be the pavement of the road to success.

Individual Exercise 6.2 *Successful Student Classroom Behavior Chart*

Purpose: One of the best ways for you to produce objective feedback on your behavior is to score yourself on a chart (see page 62). In this way you can see your progress on a daily basis and make changes just as quickly. This exercise is designed to produce the feedback/adjustment exchange that one needs to recognize and change behaviors.

Directions: Give yourself a +1 for every time you complete a behavior within the indicated time frame and a –1 for every time you fail to complete a behavior within the indicated time frame.

Closure: This exercise takes time, but it's worth it. Once these basic successful communication behaviors are learned, they can be applied in many situations.

Successful Student Classroom Behavior Chart 6.2A

Daily Behaviors

	1	2	3	4	5	6	7	8	9	10	11	12	13	14	15	16	17	18	19	20	21	**Total**

Days

on time to class

well groomed, dressed

materials read

sit near front

not talking during lecture

discussing in class

assignments on time

smile, say "hello"

eye contact

Bi-Monthly Behaviors

First 2	Second 2	Third 2	Fourth 2	Fifth 2	**Total**

Weeks

interest/questions

no "bull" handed

joke/story/anecdote

Monthly Behaviors

First	Second	Third	Fourth	**Total**

Months

show you realize the value of the class

excuse yourself for legitimate absences

make appointment

Individual Exercise 6.3 *Report on Successful Behaviors*

Purpose: This exercise is designed to help you be more conscious of your behavior—to give you feedback on how closely you are following the successful student path. If you can be conscious of your behavior and its consequences, you will easily make changes for self-improvement. Without developing consciousness of your actions, you will simply and ineffectively be sleepwalking through your life.

Directions:
1. Total your scores on the preceding charts after 21 days of class.
2. Determine which successful student behaviors you are weakest in. Also determine whether you have scored a +1 in all time frames for any successful student behaviors.
3. Write a memo to your freshman seminar professor that follows the organization outlined below:

MEMO

FROM: (*your name*)
TO: (*freshman seminar instructor's name*)
SUBJECT: (*report on Successful Student Classroom Behavior Chart*)
DATE:

Enclosed you will find charts that indicate . . .
Discuss best scores—were these consistent with or a departure from high school behaviors?
Discuss low scores—were these consistent with or a departure from high school behaviors?
Discuss how the variation in class format (size, method of instruction) affected your successful student behaviors.
State two objectives to accomplish two successful student behaviors and the date that you will act on these objectives.

Note: This memo should be typed neatly. The words on the memo are the formal communication; the neatness or sloppiness is the nonverbal communication.

Closure: The act of writing the memo should have given you an opportunity to make a detailed analysis of your classroom communication and the changes you want to make to improve it. Also, by formally stating that you are going to do something, you have committed yourself to some action. You will be more motivated to achieve your new goal.

Group Activity 6.4 *Taking a Professor to Lunch*

Purpose: Context influences communication. Outside the classroom the rules of authority and power that govern the professor–student relationship are not as pervasive. Faculty can let go a little—as long you do not start pressing them on grades. The purpose of this exercise is to help you get away from the formal context and into a more informal one with a favorite faculty member, who ideally will become a friend or mentor.

Directions:
1. Join with two other students in your freshman seminar and select a professor you would like to take to lunch, for whatever reason.
2. Determine how much you can afford, what kind of atmosphere you would like, and who will hold the money and pay the check and tip. If you are not comfortable with the restrictions of a low budget or the limitation of local cafeterias, be creative—put together a picnic.
3. Determine what lunch times would be convenient for the members of your group.
4. Delegate one of your members to invite the professor.
5. Ask the professor to extend an invitation to an upperclassman who had performed well in one or several of his or her courses. Be sure to arrange a meeting place and time—and offer to contact the upperclassman if the professor is too busy at the moment.
6. Have one of your group "touch base" with the professor the day or morning before the lunch to be sure he or she can still make it. Ask the name of the upperclassman invited.

Preparing for the Lunch
1. The best way to ensure that you will be relaxed is to have everything planned out a week in advance. When groups do things, the procrastinator can mess it up for everyone.
2. Generally, anything is fair game for conversation at the lunch. Some general topics might be:
   ❖ What makes your school special?
   ❖ Where are you from?

❖ Do you enjoy teaching?

❖ What do you expect from students?

❖ What courses do you enjoy teaching the most?

3. Feel free to talk about yourselves, what you like, what makes you nervous about being a freshman—revealing oneself is a strong communication strategy.

4. If an upperclassman joins you, ask him/her how he/she succeeded in this professor's classes, what he/she found interesting, how he/she chose a major, and so on.

Closure: Taking a faculty member to lunch is an event you rarely forget. Your energy is high, and the faculty member is usually having a good time. Most students can look back on this experience as the time they first saw a faculty member as a human being.

Group Activity 6.5 *Debriefing the Lunch*

Purpose: A proper thanks to someone who gave time for your need is always best done with a formal letter. This is true when you begin to seek interviews in your career search also.

Directions:

1. Compose a letter from the three in your group thanking the professor and the upperclassman for an enjoyable lunch. A second sentence might mention one highlight of the event from your perspective. Mail both letters and give a copy to your freshman instructor.

2. Be prepared to explain the following to the other students in your freshman seminar.

   a. Which professor did you invite and why?

   b. Where did you have the lunch and why?

   c. Who was the upperclassman invited? Did he/she attend?

   d. What topics did you discuss?

   e. What did you learn?

   f. Did you enjoy yourself? Why or why not?

   g. What would you do differently next time?

Closure: This activity should have taught you some of the secrets of a successful interview. The process does not end when the actual interview is over. Thanks are always in order and remembered when given. Reflection over the succeeding days will help you to get more and more meaning from the interview.

Individual Exercise 6.6 *Interviewing Your Professors*

Purpose:
1. To create a time and context in which you can begin to break down the barriers that naturally exist between strangers before they begin to work together.
2. To help you to begin to discover the unique role that college faculty can play in your development.
3. To help you understand the nature of the educational tradition that you became a part of when you registered as a freshman in a college or university.

Directions:
1. Select two faculty members—one you would like to talk to because you like something about him/her or his/her teaching, the second because you do not like something about him/her, the course he/she is teaching, or simply because you are afraid to talk to him/her.
2. Make an appointment to see them for half an hour, sometime between now and the next class period. Suggestion: Call today if you can—sometimes it takes a week to get together during the busy season.
3. Be sure that you write down the time, date, and place for your interview appointment.
4. To ensure that things will go smoothly, compose a two-sentence note to the professors following this general form:

(Date)

Dear_____,

    This is to confirm that we will meet in your office (room, number, building, date, day, time) so that I may conduct my freshman seminar interview assignment with you. If there are any problems, feel free to contact me at (your phone/address).
    Thank you very much for offering your time.

> Sincerely,
> (*signature*)
> (Your name typed or printed)

5. Prepare your interview by thinking about the suggested questions following these directions. Create some of your own questions as well. It is OK to come up with a question during the

interview if the professor says something that strikes your curiosity.

6. Be prepared to make mental notes (which are best preserved by writing them down just after the interview) about the nonverbal context of the interview. Refer to the nonverbal observation guides that follow the suggested questions for the faculty interview.

7. After the interviews, write or type (typing is always more professional) a report to your freshman seminar instructor, using the form provided after the nonverbal observation guides.

8. Be prepared to summarize your report in a discussion within your freshman seminar.

Questions for the Faculty Interview

1. What is the nature of a liberal arts education? How does it differ from a professional education?
2. What academic subjects interest you? Why?
3. What is your favorite hobby and what do you get out of it?
4. What is the most positive aspect that your college or university has to offer in an undergraduate education?
5. Where did you go to college? Who was your favorite professor and why?
6. If you could require me to read one thing before I leave college, what would it be and why? Where could I find it? (After you complete your interview, locate a copy of the work and page through it—at least—to locate the main idea.)
7. Compose two or three questions of your own.

Nonverbal Observation Guides

How was the office personalized: pictures, plaques, plants?

_____

_____

Did the professor sit behind a desk or openly in front of you?

_____

_____

Did the situation appear to be formal or informal? Why?

_____

_____

Was eye contact made often, smiles exchanged?

_____

_____

Did you relax more as the interview progressed? Why?

_____

_____

Other observations:

_____

_____

_____

_____

_____

_____

_____

Closure: By this time, you should feel much more comfortable talking with faculty. You should also have a much clearer perception of the educational goals and objectives of your faculty.

Faculty Interview Report Form

Your name_____   Reporting date _____/_____/_____

Professor interviewed _____   Date ___/___/___ Time:_____

Your impression of the faculty member before the interview:

_____

_____

_____

What you learned from the questions asked:

1. _____

2. _____

3. _____

4. _____

5. _____

6. _____

7. _____

Nonverbal observations:

_____

_____

_____

Your impressions of the faculty member after the interview:

_____

_____

Individual Exercise 6.7 *Giving Your Professor Some Feedback*

Purpose: Very often your professors do not know how well they are getting information across to you until exam time. Most faculty are very thankful for feedback that can help them educate you. This exercise can be a positive influence on your own education.

Directions: After at least a few weeks of class, fill out Form 6.7A for at least one of your professors and send it to them in the campus mail. Your suggestions could also be shared in discussion in your freshmen seminar.

Closure: The more you contribute to the improvement of the teaching in your classroom, the more exciting your education will be. Don't leave it all up to the faculty. Be a part of the process.

Journal Entry

Write several paragraphs on how your perceptions of faculty have changed because of the interview process in this chapter.

Teaching Effectiveness Observation and Feedback Form 6.7A

Professor's name _____

Course title _____Time taught _____

Observations made re: teaching format and style—how they affect learning

_____

_____

_____

What does the professor do in class that helps you become more interested in the subject?

_____

_____

_____

What does the professor do in class that distracts you or decreases your motivation for the subject?

_____

_____

_____

Suggestions

_____

_____

_____

❖ Chapter 7 ❖

Critical Thinking
The Mark of a Liberal Arts Education

In *College Is Only the Beginning*, Thorne Compton discusses the heart of higher education in America as learning to think as opposed to learning facts; learning to integrate ideas as opposed to answering right or wrong; and, above all, learning to enjoy life as opposed to learning to do a job. Take it seriously. For you, the nature of your higher education can make the difference between living the life of a free person and the life of the modern slave—without chains, but also without choice.

The purpose of this chapter is to give you some activities in critical thinking that follow Compton's examples. Think of these exercises and activities as games—not homework. Play with the variables. Create your own solutions and reasons.

Group Activity 7.1 *Identifying Liberal Arts in Your Education*

Purpose: You are more likely to find something if you know what you are looking for and why you should want to have it. One of the most significant functions of academic advisers, as demonstrated by Compton in *College Is Only the Beginning*, is to point out the value in various liberal arts courses for the freshman. Most high schools do not articulate the liberal arts philosophy, although many of them follow it. But as a college student it is important for you to understand *how* your education is changing you and what those changes may mean in the rest of your life.

Directions: Below are listed and defined five areas that usually compose a liberal arts education. Decide which of your courses fit into one of these five areas.

Five Areas of the Liberal Arts

1. *The arts* study human thought and behavior through the creative works of people from the earliest appearance of human beings until today.
2. *The humanities* study thought and experience through the written record of what people have thought, felt, or experienced in a variety of cultures. Subject areas include: languages and literatures, philosophy, history, religion.
3. *The social sciences* study human beings and their behavior from a variety of perspectives: as individuals (psychology) or as economic or political entities (economics and political science).
4. *Quantitative studies* create systems for describing the physical world or human behavior in abstract or mathematical terms. Includes mathematics, statistics, computer science.
5. *The sciences* study the physical world and the symbolic relationships within it.

Your Liberal Arts Courses

Course	*Area of the Liberal Arts*
1. _____	_____
2. _____	_____
3. _____	_____
4. _____	_____
5. _____	_____

Directions continued: Either alone or with other freshmen, approach a professor in one of your liberal arts courses. Ask your liberal arts professor to discuss (in small groups or, preferably, in class) the three questions that follow. Summarize the conclusions of the discussion in the space provided after the three questions. After everyone in your freshman seminar has recorded the conclusions of his/her liberal arts class discussion, the conclusions should be read aloud for the edification of all in the seminar.

Course: _____ Professor: _____

1. What is the nature of a liberal arts education?

_____

_____

_____

2. How is this course integrated into the liberal arts; that is, how do the subject matter and the thinking process in this course relate to those of other liberal arts courses?

_____

_____

_____

3. What is the value of this course to the citizen of a free society in the modern world? How does this course help us to solve our problems in society? How does this course help us to maintain and extend our freedom?

_____

_____

_____

Closure: This activity should have given you new insight into the nature of a liberal arts education and the courses that you are taking this term. The topic of discussion in liberal arts classes is not just the "what" of learning but also the "how" and "why." This kind of activity often creates a campus-wide discussion on the nature of the liberal arts. I hope, for your benefit, that such a discussion occurs in your classes.

Group Activity 7.2 *The Integration of Ideas in Liberal Arts*

Purpose: A liberal arts education prepares us to think critically and teaches us to understand ourselves, our culture, and our physical environment from a number of perspectives. The purpose of this exercise is to give you some experience in solving problems with critical thinking.

Directions for preparation: The problem presented in this activity is one we all face. Your task is *not* to provide a correct answer but rather to build on the ideas already presented until you have as many possible perspectives on the nature of the problem as one could hope for. After all, problems can be solved only after they are understood.

Read each informational selection and record three deductions or ideas that come to your mind by relating the information to the problem. Try to come up with the ideas on your own. Resort to obtaining ideas from others outside the class only if you cannot come up with enough ideas after five days of working on the task.

Directions for in-class process: Divide the chalkboard into five sections and label them according to the divisions of the liberal arts.

Nominate one member of the class to be class recorder. The recorder should place the title of the problem on the chalkboard. After summarizing the problem, the other members of the class must call out in a reasonably orderly fashion everything they can deduce or suppose from the given information while the recorder writes the ideas on the board under their proper category. All ideas that reveal more about the situation should likewise be recorded. In brainstorming, even wild and seemingly unrelated ideas should be recorded, because they help us to create new ideas.

Problem: The reduction of tension and armed conflict around the world between the Soviet Union and the United States.

Artistic information: Music and painting produced by the average citizen is folk art. It is usually a true expression of a people's perspective—how they see things and others, how they feel about events and others. Such art is usually not influenced by political propaganda.

Deductions or associated ideas:

1. _____

2. _____

3. _____

Humanities (historical) information: In the past 2,000 years the present-day heart of the Soviet Union has been overrun by invading armies dozens of times, culminating in recent years with the massive destruction and loss of life inflicted by the forces of Napoleon and Hitler. The United States has never been invaded but did militarily occupy the Soviet Union after the communist revolution.

Deductions or associated ideas:

1. _____

2. _____

3. _____

Social science (psychological) information: People in dangerous situations (like walking down a dark inner-city street at night) sometimes develop defensive strategies that may appear to be offensive in nature because a strong posture may deter attack whereas a weak posture may invite attack.

Deductions or associated ideas:

1. _____

2. _____

3. _____

Social science (economic) information: The strain of decades of large military budgets has weakened the economies of both the Soviet Union and the United States.

Deductions or associated ideas:

1. _____

2. _____

3. _____

Quantitative information: Mathematical models of games have demonstrated that games teach us how to think in certain ways. The games of a culture are in fact tools for teaching people how to approach the world and others. While we take control of the elements of our environment much like a child takes control over the pieces of a puzzle, the Soviets appear to approach their world strategies much as one would play a game of chess.

Deductions or associated ideas:

1. _____

2. _____

3. _____

Scientific information: The Soviet Union and the United States are among the most advanced countries in medical, agricultural, chemical, and biological research. Yet much of their knowledge is not shared or cooperatively applied to the problems of the world because of the fierce competition that has existed between them in recent decades.

Deductions or associated ideas:

1. _____

2. _____

3. _____

Closure: Brainstorming is one of the first stages in critical thinking. The well-educated person can gather together ideas and create new combinations just by reflecting on what he or she knows.
This exercise should have demonstrated how all the perspectives
in the liberal arts are applicable to problem solving and how
ideas can be combined from different areas to form new insights.

Group Activity 7.3 *Applying the Liberal Arts*

Purpose: The problems challenging today's college students are
much like those faced by preceding generations. Even the environmental problems, which could destroy life as we know it, were
confronted by other civilizations—on a smaller scale, of course.
Each of the areas of the liberal arts can contribute something toward eliminating war, poverty, pollution, caste, tyranny, and
disease, which have caused the demise of many past civilizations. This activity may help you apply your education to the solution of some of our greatest problems.

Directions: Have the class nominate the three problems they
consider to be challenges to the survival of our civilization. Form
a small group for each problem. Define the problem by stating in
writing: **(1)** what it looks like when it occurs; **(2)** what the imme-
diate causes are; **(3)** what social values (such as greed causing environmental damage) perpetuate the problem; and **(4)** what each
of the five categories of liberal arts courses listed in Activity 7.1
could contribute toward solving the problem. Report your conclusions to your freshman seminar professor in a two-page summary.

Closure: You may wonder about the utility of some of your liberal
arts courses when you enter college. As you proceed toward graduation, you should come to understand the nature of a liberal arts
education and why it has survived as a fundamental component of
our culture for thousands of years. The liberal arts teach us to integrate ideas so that we can bring all possible points of view to
the problems that face us individually and as a society.

Journal Entry

Below are some general course areas that are found in many colleges and universities in the United States. The general areas are divided into the five liberal arts categories and placed in **bold type** in a question. Choose at least three course areas and a question in each, locate a related course description in your college or university catalog, and respond to the question in one or two paragraphs.

Arts

How can courses in **jazz or classical music appreciation** help you develop new options in entertainment?

How can courses in the **art of a particular culture** help you understand other people in the world?

Humanities

How can courses in **literature or drama** increase your enjoyment of television or movies?

How can courses in **foreign languages** help you to see old things in new ways?

Social Science

How can courses in the **sociology of the child or adolescent** help you become a better parent?

How can courses in **politics and government** help you influence the regulations or laws of your neighborhood or town?

Quantitative Studies

How can courses that familiarize you with the **data-processing functions of computers** expand your career possibilities?

How can courses in **statistics** help you determine the credibility of various social science reports?

Science

How can courses in **environmental biology** help you understand toxic-waste issues?

How can **a chemistry lab** help you increase your problem-solving skills?

❖ Chapter 8 ❖

Logical Reasoning

The purpose of this chapter is to give you some practice in rational thinking. There is a difference between your opinion and a rational, logical conclusion. Many students confuse the two and give an off-the-cuff answer when a well developed thesis is expected. A thesis, according to Foster Tait in *College Is Only the Beginning*,[1]

> refers to something you want to prove. In any paper, the thesis is the central point—it represents what must be proved within the context of the paper. A paper without a thesis would be like a geometry with no theorems, or a work on astronomy that maintained only that a certain comet might or might not return. Such a paper would be useless. Science requires more of its practitioners, and so do teachers in any subject you can name. *A paper of any merit always states a thesis*. The thesis is always expressed as a statement, and it must be proved by correct, logical reasoning.
>
> When you present a thesis and then give reasons that it should be accepted, you almost always ensure that your sentences and paragraphs, indeed your entire paper, will progress logically. To many college professors, the most poorly reasoned papers they receive are those where nothing is being argued and a simple comparison is made. If you do make comparisons between two authors, you should do so within the context of a thesis that states what you are comparing and why that point is important to an understanding of one or more works

[1]Foster E. Tait, "How Rational Thinking Affects Student Success," in *College Is Only the Beginning* (Belmont, Calif.: Wadsworth, 1985), p. 78.

of the authors. You should then defend the thesis, which means introducing evidence to support it.

Before you write or think, consider your thesis. Statements that you make should offer evidence in support of your position. The following exercises will strengthen your capacity for rational thinking. If you do not find them to be easy, that is a good reason for doing them again in a week.

Individual Exercise 8.1 *Developing a Thesis Statement*

Purpose: This exercise presents a typical freshman experience as a thesis development problem: freshman anxiety as the subject for a paper. Although the subject may be familiar, the approach to developing the topic into a thesis may be unfamiliar. The purpose of this exercise is to give you some practice at forming a rational thesis starting with a familiar subject.

Directions: Three steps to developing a thesis statement follow. Write six responses to each question, then proceed in this book to see how I would approach the thesis development. If you look at my answers first, you will only cheat yourself.

Evidence: Where would you acquire evidence to determine whether your own or another's anxiety experience was unique or common to most freshmen?

Terms: How would you determine the terms you would use to best describe the anxiety experience and its relationship to successful performance?

Acceptability of statements: How would you determine whether your statements about the relationship between freshman anxiety and successful performance are acceptable or not?

One Response to Exercise Questions

Acquiring Evidence

1. *Survey freshman seminar and some upperclassmen.* Any survey should distinguish the respondents according to whether they

are residents or commuters, traditional age or older, male or female, from small or large families, accustomed to sharing a room or not, excited or hesitant about college, and so on. Look at a chapter of any basic book on social science research to discover why the preceding factors are important, then proceed.

2. *Ask your instructor.* Your instructor has two perspectives on the freshman experience: **(1)** Faculty were freshmen once; they followed the same basic steps that you tread now. **(2)** They have been trained to work with freshmen and have probably helped a number of other students through the passages you are now exploring. Think about what you would like to ask them. Ask them either to see you in private or to set some class time aside for a group interview. The latter approach might bring forth questions from other students that will take you beyond your own expectations.

3. *Ask Friday, Gardner, Jewler, or other experts.* Experts are sometimes hard to find, but we do have those moments when we can meet with students or spend some time on the phone. I personally believe in reading the works of experts, then writing them or calling them on the phone. A little detective work and persistence can really pay off. Experts love to talk about their subject (which in our case is you). They also travel and may be found in your area. I have interviewed and corresponded with many national and international figures just by following their travel plans and arranging an interview at their convenience.

4. *Interview your school counselor, psychologist, and so on.* These people are in the front lines with students who are battling their internal conflicts. They have a clear overview of student fears and the effects of those fears. They also have numerous strategies for overcoming these problems. In such interviews it is appropriate to discuss your own concerns, as well as other kinds of problems they have encountered (names withheld, of course).

5. *Interview your dean of students.* Most colleges and universities employ someone or several individuals who oversee the nonacademic aspects of student life. Such people are usually warm, open, and concerned. They also have considerable experience in working with freshmen transition problems.

6. *Review your library card catalog, relevant indexes, and computer search devices for articles and studies* on the subjects of student anxiety, study skills, and so on. Reference librarians are there to help you find such information. A quick review can supply you with valuable data from studies done at other universities.

Developing Terms

Developing terms involves questions of audience (who will read the thesis) as well as definitions of subjects. Choose your terms carefully and they will work for you.

1. Make a list of the terms used by the six sources in the preceding section.
2. Consult a dictionary, a thesaurus, or an encyclopedia to clarify the meaning of any words you cannot define with confidence and clarity. Make sure you can give a clear generalization accompanied by a specific example.
3. Ask students, administrators, faculty, and experts to order your list of terms according to which are most descriptive of the experience from their point of view.
4. Eliminate terms that are repetitive.
5. Categorize your terms into common and uncommon experiences.
6. Select the terms that best coincide with the examples (experiences) that you are describing.

Developing Acceptable Statements

1. Determine who will be the primary audience of your thesis. The language in any written work should be selected according to the expertise of the intended audience. An audience of poets would likely use language different from that of an audience of physicists.
2. Determine whether your statements can be verified by the evidence available to you.
3. Review. Check for fallacies: Have you used the word *all* when you should have used *most*? Basically, fallacies are incorrect reasoning from premises to conclusions. Foster Tait discusses many common fallacies in his essay quoted at the beginning of this chapter. If you are confused about fallacies, refer to that essay or to a logic textbook before proceeding.
4. Determine whether you are using the evidence from your most credible sources. Recognized experts might be the most credible (likely to be believed), while specific examples from your peers might provide local color and interesting anecdotes.

Closure: The preceding exercise was designed to give you a clear idea of the process of developing a thesis through rational thinking. If you were confused by any aspect of this exercise, tell your instructor. Once you master the rational approach to thesis development, you will be able to apply it with positive results in all of your subjects.

Group Activity 8.2 *Small-Group Thesis Statement Project*

Purpose: Some students learn concepts more easily when they see the concept applied by others. This activity can improve many students' understanding of developing a thesis through rational thinking. The previous exercise can serve as a useful guide for those involved in this activity.

Directions:
1. Form small groups of five students.
2. Have each elect to pursue one of the sources listed below.
3. In one week submit, in writing, to your freshman seminar instructor a thesis statement relating freshman anxiety to problems of successful students.

Sources:
1. Interview your instructor or an expert.
2. Read "Anxiety Management" in *College Is Only the Beginning.*
3. Interview two upperclassmen.
4. Interview two graduate students or members of the faculty.
5. Read two articles listed in the reference indexes in your library. (Ask your reference librarian for assistance.)

Closure: By working with a team, you should have been able to speed up the development of your reasoning ability. You should have been able to see how your piece of the puzzle fits into the larger picture. The feedback from your instructor should be viewed as a guidance tool for further development of your thesis.

Individual Exercise 8.3 *Identifying Fallacies*

Purpose: One of the best ways to learn rational and logical reasoning is to identify fallacies. Once you can identify fallacies quickly, you will avoid them in your work and recognize them in others' arguments.

Directions: The following list names the fallacies discussed by Foster Tait in *College Is Only the Beginning.* Below the list are statements that are examples of fallacies. Place the name of the correct fallacy in front of each statement.

Fallacies

Argument directed to the man (*argumentum ad hominem*)
Appeal to force (*argumentum ad baculum*)
Appeal to pity (*argumentum ad misericordiam*)
Appeal to authority (*argumentum ad verecundiam*)
Appeal to popularity (*argumentum ad populum*)
Argument from ignorance (*argumentum ad ignorantiam*)
False cause
Hasty generalization

Fallacy	Statement
1. _____	I can't believe that you want to take another sociology course. Just one day in Professor Isodor's class will show you how boring sociology can be.
2. _____	America and her allies won World War II because right was on our side.
3. _____	Law and business are the best majors because that's where the money is.
4. _____	My roommate recommends Survey of American History with Professor Maxwell for a profound understanding of the events and a lot of great stories.
5. _____	Are you going to believe this rubbish about heart attacks from an overweight doctor who smokes two packs a day?
6. _____	You just have to give me a good grade for your course. If I get lower than a B I'll lose my scholarship, disappoint my parents, and be compelled to take on a part-time job to pay for my tuition.
7. _____	No. What I said was that you have the option to read the required readings just as you have the option to fail the course.

Fallacy	Statement
8. _____	We have demonstrated that six ounces of vodka on the rocks, six ounces of bourbon on the rocks, or six ounces of scotch on the rocks will cause a person to become intoxicated. And we therefore conclude that ice can have an intoxicating effect on some people.
9. _____	Between the *Tibetan Book of the Dead*, the account in the Bible, and my grandfather's personal experience, I am convinced that there is life after death. Because you have not read either work or known someone who has come back, I suggest that you take my word for it.

Note: Answers are at the end of the chapter.

Closure: This exercise should have given you some practice in identifying faulty reasoning in typical statements made by people who are not using rational thinking. You should be better prepared to identify fallacies after having practiced here.

Individual Exercise 8.4 *Recording the Logic Around You*

Purpose: Your world is filled with fallacious statements. Such statements abound in most of the public electronic and print media. Because you are exposed to media often, you may find yourself reacting to false conclusions, often referred to as propaganda. If you base your decisions on false conclusions, you may get into difficulty. The purpose of this exercise is to help you be more critical of the media messages that you consume daily.

Directions: Listen or watch for and record logical and illogical statements from the sources listed on the following page. Write the statement in the space provided along with a brief explanation of why it is logical or fallacious.

Sources	Logical statement	Fallacious statement
U.S. President	_____	_____
	_____	_____
Explanation:	_____	_____
	_____	_____
Ad in newspaper	_____	_____
	_____	_____
Explanation:	_____	_____
	_____	_____
Commercial on TV	_____	_____
	_____	_____
Explanation:	_____	_____
	_____	_____
Your choice: Discussion with roommate or friend	_____	_____
	_____	_____
Explanation:	_____	_____
	_____	_____
Discussion with your parents	_____	_____
	_____	_____
Explanation:	_____	_____
	_____	_____

Closure: This exercise should have demonstrated some of the fallacies that you are exposed to daily. Learn to watch for them. Knowing whether a statement is sound or not is the sign of the well-educated person.

Answers to fallacy questions: 1. hasty generalization; 2. false cause; 3. appeal to popularity; 4. appeal to authority; 5. argument directed to the man; 6. appeal to pity; 7. appeal to force; 8. false cause; 9. argument from ignorance

Journal Entry

Write an essay explaining how you are either a logical or emotional thinker.

❖ Chapter 9 ❖

Majors and Careers in Your Time

I once read a book entitled *Jung and the Story of Our Time* by Laurens Van der Post. I was fascinated by the author's concept of each time having a life of its own. The life experiences of people in the Bronze Age, the Stone Age, the early Middle Ages, the Industrial Age were all very different insofar as the beliefs, fears, values, and political and atmospheric climates differed. As I looked at the life of my time, I began to realize that there was something special about my generation. We were born in the years following World War II, a period of unparalleled optimism born out of a triumph over the threat of world domination, death, and destruction. Our parents were bonded by their experience either in the military or in support of the war effort. They had shared the same challenge, faced the same fears, celebrated the same victories. Their heroes were world heroes, whose recognition was international, whose power was without measure. In the decade following the war, our parents rebuilt the ravaged world through the Marshall Plan and economic and political alliances that reshaped the organization of the world into much of what it is today.

We grew up in a time when confidence and unlimited expansion and opportunity were assumed to be the nature of things. And in addition to this atmosphere, there was "we." We, the war babies, were a massive bulge in the population, who year by year moved through our society changing everything in our path. My grade school expanded to twice its size to accommodate us, as the scramble to find teachers became a national quest. We became accustomed to re-creating society as we grew. We assumed that we had the power to define what we wanted, because our concerns and our needs were often taken into consideration in the design of our institutions—from a very expanded Boy Scouts to a geometric expansion in post-secondary education. And when the Vietnam War came, we gave our opinions on that, too.

For many of us, the questions that you face regarding career, values, and goals were not our questions. We did not have to face such questions because we lived in a world of endless opportunity. Your world and the life of your time differ considerably from the days of our emergence into society. I always respond to the question of how I arrived at where I am today by stating that I fell back on the path of least resistance. We did not have the benefits of career counseling or professional academic advising way back in the '60s. We just had a philosophy of "do your own thing," and many of us took that seriously. The exercises and activities that follow are representative of contemporary career counseling tactics and strategies for defining and doing your own thing. That is, they begin to answer the question: How can I be myself and be a success?

Group Activity 9.1 *The Life of Your Time*

Purpose: It is valuable to talk about the life of your time. In doing so you will discover what a great mahatma once called the "great dream dreaming us." Learn to recognize the mythologies and dreams that guide the life of your time. Eventually you will come to know the silent currents in your social ocean. You will learn to navigate, set your course for distant horizons, and land safely upon the shore of your choice.

If you do not recognize the forces acting on you, you will act but not know why. For example, the concept of success that most freshmen bring to college is self-oriented and often economic in nature. Few freshmen tell me that they want to preserve the world for the next generation. At this time in our history, our society is pushing one concept over the other, and when society pushes, you move—until you learn to make your own decisions.

The purpose of this exercise is to help you, with the assistance of your peers, to identify the push, the forces that are in our society at present. In this way, you can begin to distinguish your decisions from social trends.

Directions:
1. Form into small groups of no more than five to a group with the instructor joining one of the groups and a student monitoring the timing of the stages of the activity. Each group should have about ten minutes to list all the forces that influence their major and career decisions, an example of how it occurs in their lives, and whether it is a positive or negative force (that is, does it feel good or bad to have this force acting on you?). A force can be anything from the spirit of your time to a specific parental or economic pressure. If you perceive it, consider it to be real.
2. After each group has completed phase one, the results should be summarized on flip charts or the chalkboard. When the summaries are completed, a representative from each group should explain the details of the discussion behind the summaries. As the discussion proceeds, each class member should make two lists out of the information: **(a)** the forces that influence your decision-making process and **(b)** the forces that do not influence your decision-making process. Hold on to these lists.

Closure: By now you should have some idea of the forces that have influenced and will continue to influence your decisions. Awareness of these forces will give you more control over them.

Individual Exercise 9.2 *Your Personality/ Your Career*[1]

Purpose: Too many students elect a major and career because someone told them that jobs will be plentiful in a particular area. In the '70s there was a stampede toward schools of engineering; later the crowd headed for computer science. I could see the trend change every three or four years, but the reasoning was always the same: "I want to major in _____ because there are jobs in _____." A person who determines his or her life direction in this fashion will probably not succeed as well as the person who plots a life course by the strengths and needs of his or her very individual personality. When your career matches your personality, you will love your work, come up with creative ideas, and solve problems that only perplex those in the herd.

This exercise will help you identify some dominant aspects (strengths and needs) of your personality and then find success areas for people like yourself.

Directions: Review the six personality themes and related career fields that are described in this exercise. Circle words, phrases, and careers that appeal to you. After the descriptions you will find a space to write in your dominant theme and two subthemes. In the dominant theme space, enter the theme that best describes the way you perceive yourself. Then write in three phrases from the dominant theme description that you would feel comfortable using to describe your personality. Feel free to make up phrases in addition to the ones in the description. Do the same for the two subthemes.

Another way to see how you relate to a theme is to review the career areas that follow the theme descriptions. The careers represent the kinds of work that people from that particular theme find rewarding and satisfying.

1.   Realistic Theme

Realistic people see themselves as competitive, assertive, responsible, down-to-earth, straightforward, athletic, and stable. They prefer to work in mechanical or scientific areas rather than cultural or artistic areas. Unlike those who prefer to work in theoretical areas, realistic people apply their above-average physical strength and coordination to the solution of problems.

[1]Adapted and reproduced by special permission from *The Self-Directed Search Manual*, by John L. Holland, Ph.D. Copyright 1978. Published by Consulting Psychologist Press, Inc. Palo Alto, CA 94306.

Realistic Theme Career Areas: barber, fish and wild life manager, dairy farmer, gem cutter, laboratory technician, heavy equipment operator, military officer, skilled worker, health and safety inspector, ship's captain, television repair person

2. Investigative Theme

Investigative people prefer logical reasoning to action. They tend to be good at producing a systematic analysis of a task. Although their outward appearance is reserved, they tend to be liberal thinkers. They prefer to work alone rather than in a group.

Investigative Theme Career Areas: city planner, medical doctor, psychologist, theoretical physicist, marine biologist, flight engineer, laboratory researcher, science writer, logician, sanitation engineer, detective

3. Artistic Theme

Artistic people like to work alone in creative environments, value self-expression and physical tasks that do not require great strength. They tend to express their emotions more than most people and like to develop original ideas. These people like cultural events. Their disorderly and nonconforming ways are less compatible with the sciences than with cultural and aesthetic endeavors.

Artistic Theme Career Areas: writer, composer, cartoonist, graphic illustrator, photographer, poet, performer, magazine illustrator, book editor, advertising consultant, department store window designer, studio artist, landscape architect, stained glass designer/builder

4. Social Theme

These people like to work with other people. Social people are good interpersonal communicators who are often found in the teaching and helping professions. They often have command of the language and enjoy working with small discussion groups, but they tend to avoid athletic activity or machinery.

Social Theme Career Areas: teacher, marriage counselor, school superintendent, rehabilitation counselor, events coordinator, youth development officer, theater manager, group counselor, speech and hearing therapist, academic advisor, service club organizer, orientation director, task force coordinator, school board member, politician

5. Enterprising Theme

People who perceive themselves as enterprising have a strong command of the language and utilize it in a dynamic way to persuade others rather than to support the needs of others. They possess a good sense of leadership and the drive to get to the top of their profession. Enterprising people prefer to oversee an entire project and delegate the detail work to others. They also place a high value on material wealth.

Enterprising Theme Career Areas: public relations director, sales and promotion executive, politician, media newscaster, mayor, hospital administrator, travel guide, invention marketeer, direct dial salesperson, insurance and investment broker, department store manager, personnel manager

6. Conventional Theme

These people do well in work that has definite guidelines. They prefer order, use language well, but tend to have less physical strength than realistic people. Conventional people avoid close interpersonal relationships and ambiguity. They place a high value on material wealth.

Conventional Theme Career Areas: tax accountant, bookkeeper, statistician, traffic engineer, census counter, office clerk, hospital intake interviewer, custodian, legal secretary, physician's assistant, library staff worker, office manager, inventory controller, court clerk, parts assembler, postal worker, reservations clerk, word processor operator

My dominant theme is:_____

Phrases that best describe me from the perspective of this theme are:

_____

_____

_____

My first subtheme is:_____

Phrases that best describe me from the perspective of this theme are:

_____

_____

_____

My second subtheme is: _____

Phrases that best describe me from the perspective of this theme are:

_____

_____

_____

Closure: The themes described in this exercise are based on a model developed by John Holland, a psychologist at Johns Hopkins University. This model is not to be used as a quick way to determine your personality and compatible career choice. Rather, the model suggests possible conflicts or compatibility between career fields that you feel might be interesting. If your themes are close to each other in the model, they are compatible. If your themes are spread around the model, you might want to discuss the potential conflicts with your college's career counselor.

Holland's Hexagon

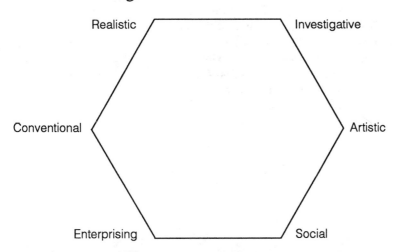

Individual Exercise 9.3 *Functional Skills Résumé*[2]

Purpose: When you begin to network—to ask around about careers and where someone like you can fit in—you should have a written description of your skills. In the world of careers, we refer to functional skills such as writing, presenting to groups, organizing notes, word processing, and so on. This exercise will guide you through the process of constructing a functional skills résumé. This will take time. Allow several weeks for writing and rewriting. Sometimes reflection or feedback from others is more important than sitting at a desk and writing. The standard good résumé goes through four or five revisions before the final form. Take your time and enjoy.

Directions:
1. List all paid and volunteer work-related experiences for the past three years.
2. List all club, community service, and church activities, including membership and offices held in high school clubs and organizations.
3. Categorize each activity according to the functional skills area that it could fall into. Each experience or activity may be assigned to several functional skills categories. For instance, president of the drama club may be designated as leadership skills, organization and management skills, and public relations skills.
4. Once all your experiences and activities have been analyzed in terms of functional skills, patterns will begin to emerge that clearly indicate strengths in certain functional skills areas.
5. Choose three areas of functional skills (things that you do well, like researching, reading, speaking, solving puzzles, cooking, creating order, persuading, drawing, leading, caring for others, motivating) to use on the résumé. Present two or three experiences and/or activities for each of the three functional skill areas selected. Try to choose functional skill areas and experiences and activities that relate to the career objective. However, this may not be possible to any great extent.
6. Follow the format used in the sample functional skills résumé. Pay close attention to the wording of each experience or activity. Begin each item with strong action words.

---

[2]*Source:* Sandra D. Branyon, "Benefits Students Gain from Writing Functional Skills Résumés" and "Instructions for Writing a Functional Skills Résumé." Reprinted by permission of the author.

7. Conclude the résumé with:

    EDUCATION

    The University of _____

    Anticipated date of graduation: _____

    Major field of study may be indicated, but it is not necessary.

8. Do not specify references.
9. Résumés should be typed, letter perfect, and centered on the page.

Closure: A few weeks after starting this exercise you should have your own functional skills résumé. Have copies printed and use it—especially in Exercise 9.6.

Example of a Functional Skills Résumé

Name
Address
Area code — phone here

Career Interest

Industrial Technology

Technical and Mechanical Skills

Operated industrial photography equipment and computerized typesetting machines while employed as specialty artist at Image Cards and Mailing, Inc., 3052 33rd Street, Airport Industrial Park, Fort Pierce, Fla. 33450, June–August, 1983.

Demonstrated sophisticated photography equipment and home entertainment systems while employed as a saleswoman at Luria's, 2045 S. U.S. #1, Fort Pierce, Fla. 33450, November–January, 1985.

Innovative and Artistic Skills

Designed logos and various advertising designs for resort corporations and business identification purposes while employed as specialty artist at Image Cards and Mailing, Inc., 3052 33rd Street, Airport Industrial Park, Fort Pierce, Fla. 33450, June–August, 1983.

Implemented artistic techniques in designing major advertising campaigns while employed as secretary at Jernigan Realty, 1010 S. U.S. #1, Fort Pierce, Fla. 33450, April–December, 1985.

Organizational/Planning Skills

Handled systematically the purchasing orders for major engine and bus components while employed as part-time secretary to Southeast Regional Purchasing Agent at Trailways, Inc., 104 Harris Street, N.W., Atlanta, Ga. 30313, December, 1983–February, 1984.

Coordinated the daily running of an up-and-coming real estate office while employed as secretary at Jernigan Realty, 1010 S. U.S. #1, Fort Pierce, Fla. 33450, April–December, 1985.

Education

University of West Florida
Pensacola, Florida 32514
Major: Industrial Technology
Minor: Physics
Anticipated date of graduation:
May, 1989

References available upon request

Individual Exercise 9.4 *Building Network/Career Options*

Purpose: Between 60 and 70 percent of all jobs are found through networking. Build your network of contacts early. This exercise will show you how to start building a career-search network from your present social network.

Directions: Below write three selected themes from Exercise 9.2 with the key phrases that best describe you:

Themes:

1. _____

2. _____

3. _____

Interview three people who do not know you well and two who do. Ask them to suggest or create a career for someone who follows the first two and possibly all three themes. One of those you ask must be a faculty member and another should be a career counselor or your adviser. At least half of those you ask should be college-educated. Show them your functional skills résumé if it is completed.

Write a thank-you note to each interviewee within 24 hours after the interview. Write a memo to your instructor and your academic adviser summarizing the results of the interviews, especially indicating all career options you are now considering.

Closure: Although this kind of interview is brief and relatively informal, you should have begun to get a feeling for the interview situation. You might have also noticed that most people came up with some new ideas for applying their skills or new contacts. This is the value of networking: Two heads are better than one.

Group Activity 9.5 *Expanding Your View*

Purpose: This activity is short but valuable. By hearing the experiences that others are having with their interviews, you will learn new questions to ask, find new career ideas, see new communication styles in action, discover new functional skills.

Listen to your peers and learn.

Directions: As the instructor receives the memos from Exercise 9.4, the students should be asked to make a brief summary presentation to the class. Those who have not yet concluded the exercise should be asked for an update on where they are in the process, what problems they are having, and when they expect to conclude.

Closure: In addition to learning new career ideas, you should have found yourself clarifying your own experience while talking. Sometimes the pressure of talking to a group causes us to come up with more to say. That is part of learning to make public presentations.

Individual Exercise 9.6 *Networking Your Career*

Purpose: This is the ultimate in the career search. Most of my students come back from this exercise with new ideas for courses to take, clearer ideas for internships, careers, more confidence in themselves and their direction in life—not to mention a support network out there waiting to help them.

Directions: Based on the feedback from the preceding exercises, activities, and your own feelings, select a career that you think you might be interested in exploring. Find at least one person with that career or at least someone who can introduce you to that person. Make a 20-minute appointment to find out the realities of that person's career. Ask such questions as: What do you do in your position? What do you like about it? What are the things you dislike about your work? What should one study to prepare for a career like yours? What skills should one have in a career like yours? Reveal some of your skills and interests and ask: Do you think that your kind of career is something that I would be happy doing? Do you know anyone else I could talk to about this career area?

Send a thank-you note within 24 hours and a memo to your instructor and your academic adviser detailing the results of the interview and stating what impact the networking might have on your overall academic plan.

Closure: If you involved yourself in this exercise, you are well on your way to defining your direction and getting involved with your personal development on a level that you never thought of before. Guide yourself with ethics; use satisfaction as your career criterion.

Journal Entry

Reflect on the process of self-examination and networking in this chapter and write several paragraphs defining your logical and emotional reactions to the process.

❖ Chapter 10 ❖

Writing Your Own Success Story

In *College Is Only the Beginning* (1989), Carolyn Matalene describes how you can improve your grade-point average by writing well. By employing private and public writing, Matalene demonstrates how to strengthen your grasp of ideas in lectures, textbooks, novels, history, and so on.

Writing takes time to learn, but your mind is growing with every new word, phrase, sentence, paragraph, and essay that you create. I remember my early days of writing when I hated to come to the end of the page for fear that I could not think of enough to fill another one. Now, I think of the first draft of a chapter as a two-day project!

The purpose of this chapter is to present a number of exercises and activities that can improve your writing as well as your performance in college. Just a little bit of work each day can make a hard task easier. Persevere and enjoy!

Individual Exercise 10.1 *Reflecting on Your Reading*

Purpose: In her first suggested exercise, Carolyn Matalene asks you to read a chapter in a text and react to a number of questions.

Such learning activities are important because the more senses that you involve in wrestling with ideas, the more you are going to retain. For example, reading aloud helps you remember, and associating the sweet smell of a pie baking with a hard-to-remember fact will make it unforgettable.

The purpose of this exercise is to help you explore a chapter in one of your textbooks from several perspectives. The more points of view you have on something, the better you will understand it and remember it.

Directions: Acquire a notebook. Choose a chapter in one of your textbooks. Review the questions at the end of the chapter. Take note of new words or concepts that are in the chapter. Read it sitting at a desk with good lighting and no distractions. When you are finished reading, close your book and respond to the following questions and statements.

1. Write a brief summary of the chapter and then proceed to the next question.
2. While you were reading you had some thoughts and reactions to the material. List as many of these thoughts and reactions as you can.
3. What did the chapter have to give to you—that is, what's important in the chapter to the field of study and how can knowing this help you?
4. Supply examples from your own experience that you could use to support the author's main ideas.
5. Can you come up with some ways to cast doubt on the author's position?
6. What was the hardest idea to understand?
7. Return to the chapter and outline the logical steps the author took to explain the difficult idea.
8. If you did not like something about the chapter, explain your reaction in your most expressive prose or poetry.
9. Take on the role of your professor and ask the questions he or she would ask. Write them down.

Closure: The first thing you have to do to learn through writing is get involved in the subject from many directions. Relate your life to it, love it, reject it, and/or use it. If you look at a house only from the front and at a distance, you will know little about it. But if you walk through it, seeing rooms where life's functions are carried on by a family, you suddenly know much more about the house, the people, and yourself. If you listen to the judgments that you make about others, you will enter another level of thought.

Individual Exercise 10.2 *Developing Comparisons*

Purpose: Aside from the fact that comparison questions frequently turn up on exams, there is another reason to practice making comparisons. When we compare things, we must isolate the comparable elements of each object or idea. In simple comparisons we may look at size, weight, color, and so on. More complex comparisons may involve evaluations of style, logic, conflicting philosophies, or moral and legal codes. In learning to make comparisons it is best to begin with the simplest level and venture toward the more complex. The following exercise will help you do just that.

Directions: Go to the nearest parking lot and select two vehicles that interest you for any reasons you choose. Respond to the following statements or questions using your observations of the two vehicles as your basis.

1. Write a simple description comparing the two vehicles by weight, length, height, closeness to the ground, and three other points of comparison.
2. Compare the colors of each vehicle using the colors of fruits and vegetables as your standard.
3. Write a commercial comparing the vehicles, consistently favoring one over the other.
4. Deduce from the style, condition, image, and value of the vehicles what the owners are like. Write two lists comparing the lifestyle and values of the owners of the vehicles.

Closure: Once you develop a sense of comparison, you will find yourself writing comparisons with ease. Always remember to list the comparative elements first with their attributes. The rest of the writing is easy.

Group Activity 10.3 *Arguing Cause and Effect*

Purpose: Much of our empirical culture is built on the understanding of cause-effect relationships in the natural environment.[1] For example, the brakes on a car work because of the relationship of friction to motion. When we understand a cause-effect relationship, we can apply it in our lives. The first step is to get yourself thinking about things in terms of cause and effect. Writing about

[1]For more on cause and effect, see Foster E. Tait, "How Rational Thinking Affects Student Success," in *College Is Only the Beginning* (Belmont, Calif.: Wadsworth, 1985, 1989).

cause and effect can help you sharpen your ability to think in this manner. This activity will exercise your cause-effect thinking.

Directions: Have members of your class nominate several different kinds of problems that they would like to know more about. You might want to choose a political issue (like the Iran–Contra affair), a health problem (like AIDS), a social problem (like divorce), or a personal problem (like honesty in relationships). Divide the class into small groups (no more than five in a group) according to who is interested in which problem.

Each group should follow the discussion agenda and report their conclusions to the class. The process should take about 20 minutes in several class periods spread over two weeks.

Cause–Effect Discussion Agenda

1. List all the examples of the problem that you can observe.
2. From your first list you will create a second listing. On a sheet of paper make a small left column and a large right column. Label the left column *cause* and the right *effect*. List the causes on the left with the effects very briefly described on the right. The description on the right could lead you to another cause *if* there is a relationship between them.
3. After your group has exhausted their personal knowledge on the subject, each group member should look up one article or report on the problem. You might want to refer to Chapter 11 on library research. After each person has researched one item, try to expand your cause–effect list.
4. Finally, determine whether you have listed all the contributing causes of the problem by answering the following questions in group discussion:
   a. How do the values of the people causing or being affected by the problem support the existence of the problem?
   b. What values, if accepted as new guides for actions, would help break the chain of cause–effect relationships that we see as a problem?
   c. How would a people's actions differ with new values, and what effect would this have on the chain of events you have outlined?
5. Now you are ready to write. Each member of the group should write a short essay on:
   a. the problem that your group discussed.
   b. what you learned about cause–effect relationships.
   c. the learning process that took place in the small group.
   d. how the personalities in your group caused the outcome of your discussion.

6. Your group should meet one final time to discuss each essay as a point of view on the problem and on the group dynamics.

Closure: If you are writing anything worth reading the preparation usually takes as long as or longer than the writing. The more you prepare with some of the basic organizing steps like discussion and outlining used in this activity, the more likely you are to write intelligently when you sit down to the task.

Individual Exercise 10.4 *Getting into History*

Purpose: The two weakest areas of American college students today are their writing skills and a sense of history. My international students consistently display a much greater knowledge of our history than do my U.S.–born students. This exercise is designed to help you develop your writing skills along with a sense of history.

Directions: Select a moment or personality in history that interests you. Collect a few sources that can give you some insight into the human experience of the time, the event, and the people involved. Choose one of the following assignments and start writing.

1. You are a relative or friend of the central figure in the historical moment. Write a short story that illustrates what it was like knowing, talking with, and helping this person during this time. Be whimsical, dramatic, or tragic—but be historically accurate.
2. You are a TV reporter transported to the historical moment. Write the script for a half-hour broadcast on the event, complete with interviews with the main personalities. Include actual quotes, facts, cause-effect discussion, and so on.
3. You are a renowned social critic who has the astounding luck to have lived for several thousand years. From your own experience, compare a modern situation (problem) with one that you lived through in your earlier years.

Closure: Most people remember best by association. If you personalize history, you may develop a better sense of the people and their times. Perhaps you will become another James Michener.

Individual Exercise 10.5 *Writing a "Great Persons" Letter*

Purpose: Sometimes the best way to get familiar with a great thinker's ideas is to put them in your words. The purpose of this exercise is to give you some practice at doing just that.

Directions: Select a person of achievement like Socrates, Jesus, Gandhi, King, Freud, Jung, Wordsworth, Nietzsche, Eleanor Roosevelt, Churchill, Mother Teresa, Shirley Chisholm, Gloria Steinem, Woody Allen, or one of your choice. Select any topic from items at the supermarket to the philosophical clash between East and West. You are now the great thinker you had selected. Write three letters on the topic: one to your mom or dad, one to a close friend, and one to your child who is now going off to college.

Closure: What we say has a lot to do with who we are saying it to. Point of view, perspective, and social status or hierarchy determine the forms of address that we use. Many great thinkers had a hard time explaining themselves to their own parents, which may have given them practice for explaining themselves to more objective audiences.

Journal Entry

Write an entry that discusses the kinds of writing that you like the best and why you like it. Be sure to give yourself a chance to create an enjoyable writing experience.

❖ Chapter 11 ❖

Your College Library
Resources for Success

In *College Is Only the Beginning*, Charles Curran shows you how to use one of your greatest resources for success: the library. The accumulated thoughts of millions of people reside within the walls of your library. The more you partake of their views of the world and the human condition, the more you will see, hear, and understand the world around you.

You don't see anything if you don't have a word for it. I used to think that weeds in my garden were just weeds. But once I studied them, I found out that the kinds of weeds in the garden will tell me whether my soil is acid or alkaline, wet or dry, sandy or heavy or rich. A little research told me that lamb's quarter, yellow dock, young dandelion leaves, purslane, chickweed, land cress, and sorrel all have two to three times the nutritional value of spinach or Swiss chard.

The purpose of this chapter is to give you some basic experience in using your library so that you don't go through life thinking of the unfamiliar as just another weed. When you select a topic for the exercises in this chapter, I suggest that you work only with something that you find personally interest-

108

ing. Either a hobby or what I call entertainment research (something you always wondered about) are good topics to use. The hard work of the step-by-step searching will fade as your sense of wonder grows. In time you will be able to quicken your research pace so that more demanding topics will be easier and more exciting.

Individual Exercise 11.1 *Basic Library Exploration*

Purpose: Every student should be able to use some general resources in order to become an educated person. The purpose of this exercise is to help you discover these resources if you don't already know them. I consider them all vital to student success. Most of these resources are standard references used by business, education, and professional people. Let's get started on developing your success resources.

Directions: Choose a topic(s) of interest to you. To get the best results, pick something that has some history to it, or at least has not occurred in the past three months. Take the form Library Exploration 11.1A to your library and look for each "search target" using the "resource" listed. Enter your comments on the information that you found in the column provided.

Closure: You should have a better sense of some of the library resources available to you when you are researching a topic and the quick and simple information gathering that you can do with your library resources.

Library Exploration Exercise 11.1A

Search Target	Resource	Comments on Information
Books related to your topic	*Cumulative Book Index*	
Newspaper coverage of a recent news event	*New York Times Index*	
Bibliography on topic (great for term papers)	*Bibliographic Index*	
Books currently available on topic for purchase	*Books in Print*	
Pamphlets (up-to-date, not easily located)	*Vertical File Index*	
Listing of related subjects (extensiveness of subject's dimensions)	Library of Congress subject headings (Check volume or card catalog)	
Items produced by U.S. government (books, magazines, brochures)	Monthly catalog of Government Documents	
Significant government reports of interest to the public (such as hearings, papers on toxic waste/AIDS, and so on)	*Public Affairs Information Service Bulletin*	

Individual Exercise 11.2 *The Subject Guide*

Purpose: There are many places to go in a library to discover what is available on the subject you are researching. Some sources will appear to be self-contained, like an encyclopedia with its condensed entries. Look for the bibliography at the end of the entry, or key people, events, and places mentioned. All could be new areas for you to research. The purpose of this exercise is to give you an opportunity to use ten basic subject guides. Don't feel that you have to do them all in one day. Research is always cumulative and often improves with reflection, additional reading, and networking.

Directions: Choose a subject that interests you—either a hobby or something that you have always wondered about. Enter the subject at the top of Subject Guide 11.2A and proceed to your library. Select at least one source from each category of sources, locate it, use it, and make a brief note on your findings in the space provided under "content note." There are many other kinds of sources besides those listed under "examples." **Note:** the *Guide to Reference Books*[1] can supply you with information about what can be found in all the various reference books in your library.

Closure: If you completed your search in this exercise, you should be much more knowledgeable on your subject than you were when you began. You should be able to construct a fairly substantial research paper with what you have gathered thus far. Moreover, knowledge once gained is forever yours.

[1]Eugene P. Sheehy, ed., *Guide to Reference Books*, 10th ed. (Chicago: American Library Association, 1986).

Subject Guide 11.2A

Subject you wish to search

Source	Example of Source	Your Source	Content Note
General encyclopedia	Encyclopaedia Britannica		
Subject area encyclopedia	Encyclopedia of World Art/ Encyclopedia of American History/Encyclopedia of Educational Research		
Journal index	Art Index/Chemical Abstracts/ Nursing Index/Sociological Abstracts/Readers' Guide to Periodical Literature		
Yearbook	World Almanac/Statesman's Yearbook/Europa Yearbook/ Statistical Abstracts of the U.S.		
Computer search	ERIC or as your library subscribes		

Subject Guide 11.2A (continued)

		Subject you wish to search	
Source	Example of Source	Your Source	Content Note
Handbooks	Bartlett's Familiar Quotations/ Famous First Facts/Concordance to the Bible		
Biographical resources (for persons)	Current Biography/Biography Index/Who Was When/Who Knows What		
Government information	Congressional Record/ Government Organizational Manual		
Laws	United States Code/Federal Register		
Directory	Encyclopedia of Associations/ Research Centers Directory		

Individual Exercise 11.3 *Career Preparation*

Purpose: Most people think that the place to find out about careers is the career library on campus. This is true for specific career information like annual reports and background information, where to network, how to interview, and so on. But if you want to know what people in your field are actually doing and what they need to know to do it successfully, you should go to your main library and/or any specialized libraries in your field. This exercise is designed to help you develop a deeper sense of what is really going on in your field(s) of interest and how you can fit in.

Directions:
1. Locate the *Subject Index* for your library and look up your career interest area(s). Several copies are usually available in your library's reference area. It tells you which key words to use when looking up your subject in other indexes, your card catalog, computer bank, and other sources.
2. List all the key words that sources on your interest area(s) are filed under.
3. Over the course of the term, set aside two hours a week. Using the resources discovered in Exercises 11.1 and 11.2 and your key words, locate information on your career interest. By the end of the term you will be ready to converse with experts in the field, because you will have a good idea of some of the major issues and leaders in your area(s).

Closure: Some things just take time. Don't be one of the instant generation who think they get the news from a half-hour broadcast in the evening. Acquiring the basics of a higher education takes four years of classes. The rest of higher education is a lifetime of being informed. Start now. Do a little here and a little there. Soon you will have command of the ideas in your field and you will be ready to contribute to the next level of development.

Individual Exercise 11.4 *Intellectual Power Development Checklist*

Purpose: There are certain learning behaviors that successful people usually develop in college. Many of these behaviors are related to library research. Through these strategies, successful people become masters of their field. They become known as the people to ask if you want to know. And to gain that status all they had to do was keep learning.

The purpose of this exercise is to give you a checklist of the behaviors to rate yourself as a success-bound researcher. Also, use this list to guide yourself in the development of your research strategies

Directions: Check the items in the following list if you already incorporate them in your research strategy. Plan to incorporate the unchecked items as soon as possible.

Successful Research Strategy Checklist

1. _____ I have reviewed the filing rules used in the college library catalog and have reviewed the available indexes in my interest area.
2. _____ I have read the rules and regulations in the library guide.
3. _____ I have examined or prepared a diagram of library areas of interest to me, including additional libraries in my geographical area.
4. _____ I have located the library section that has materials I might need on how to research and write a term paper.
5. _____ I have become acquainted with the physical arrangement of books and nonbook material in the library.
6. _____ I have used the college library for reading purposes, class assignments, and leisure.
7. _____ I have sought the expertise of librarians when my unfamiliarity with library resources required their assistance.
8. _____ I have used or examined ten of the general and specific library materials mentioned in Curran's chapter on libraries in *College Is Only the Beginning.*
9. _____ I have participated in or planned my own tour of the college library and other libraries in my geographical area.
10. _____ I have learned to use computers to search for information.
11. _____ I have learned to send for free government publications.
12. _____ I have learned what can be acquired through interlibrary loan.

Closure: The items listed in this exercise take time to do. You will never have more time for adopting them as your personal success strategies than you do now. Begin today.

Journal Entry

In a few paragraphs, explore your attitude toward library research. If you avoid it, figure out why. Is what you do while you are avoiding successful student behaviors going to give you the intellectual power you will need to succeed? Discuss this with yourself. Be your own coach and get yourself on a winning game plan.

❖ Chapter 12 ❖

Values
Guides for Action

In *College Is Only the Beginning* (1989), Richard L. Morrill discusses the origin of our values and the role they play in our lives. Morrill contends that attitudes, feelings, beliefs, and ideas qualify as genuine values only when we consciously choose them. If you act as you have been taught to act, your actions are being guided by another's values. If, after deep introspection and evaluation of alternative choices, you elect to follow either a value taught to you or one opposed to those taught to you, your actions will be guided by your own values.

This chapter will lead you through three levels of values acquisition: **(1)** understanding some of the origins of your values—especially those related to your choice to go to your college; **(2)** investigating the consequences of values in action; and **(3)** determining which values are most important to you.

Individual Exercise 12.1 *The Origin of Some of Your Values*

Purpose: As Morrill observed, your college experience is a "time for locating and testing (your) values by tracing their full implications through comparison with those of other people, by analyzing and giving voice to them." In this exercise you will focus on your values and those of your family in order to clarify how those values guided your actions when you applied to and entered your college. Then you can proceed to Group Activity 12.2 to learn how your values compare with those of your peers.

Directions: Complete the following statements after reflecting on and possibly discussing them with family or close friends for clarification.

Family Values Toward Higher Education

1. My father's formal education terminated at the _____ level.

2. My mother's formal education terminated at the _____ level.

3. My father would give the following three reasons for (*check one*)
   ❏ supporting my decision to go to this college:
   ❏ not supporting my decision to go to this college:

   _____

   _____

   _____

4. My mother would give the following three reasons for (*check one*)
   ❏ supporting my decision to go to this college:
   ❏ not supporting my decision to go to this college:

   _____

   _____

   _____

5. Higher education (*check one*) ❏ is ❏ is not a tradition in my extended family.

6. If I had complete freedom to do anything I wanted to do this year, I would

   _____

7. The decision for me to go to this college was_____% my parents' decision and
    _____% my decision.

8. My responses to Statements 6 and 7 indicate that I (*check one*)
    ❏ feel that I have complete freedom and want to go this college.
    ❏ don't feel that I have complete freedom but still want to go to this college.
    ❏ don't feel that I have complete freedom and don't really want to go to this college.

9. The reasons that I have stated to others for my choosing this college are (in the order of
    their importance to you):

    a._____

    b._____

    c._____

    d._____

10. If the above reasons do not reflect the reality of your situation (for example, finances,
    grades, need to be near home), state the real reason(s) below:

    a._____

    b._____

11. The reasons that I have stated to others for my interest in _____ as my par-
    ticular field of study are:

    a._____

    b._____

    c._____

    d._____

12. If the above reasons do not reflect the reality of your situation (for example, don't know
    but feel a need to know, have not met qualifications for your dream career, lack courage
    to go for it), state the real reasons below:

    a._____

    b._____

13. Below is a list of 16 reasons for going to college.[1] Rate the reasons from 1 (most influential in your decision) to 16 (least influential in your decision).

___To be exposed to new ideas or experiences   ___To get a degree
___To prepare for job or profession   ___To please parents
___To gain problem-solving skills   ___To assimilate knowledge
___To gain prestige or status   ___To have something to do
___To prepare for good citizenship   ___To learn how to learn
___To raise economic status   ___To find a spouse or a mate
___To gain more maturity   ___To make friends
___To be a productive member of society   ___To have fun

14. List the six key words out of all the preceding responses that name the values (yours or those of others) which have guided you into the role of a freshman at your college. Then write one paragraph about each value describing the actions that you took under the guidance of the particular value, concluding with a statement about how comfortable you are with your present life course.

a. _____   d. _____

b. _____   e. _____

c. _____   f. _____

Closure: The purpose of this exercise is to get you started on an introspective examination of the values that have guided you into your present social role as a freshman at your college. Look around the world through books, movies, newspapers, TV news, conversations with international students and discover what people your age are doing at this moment. Their actions are your minimum options. You arrived at your actions through your cultural guidance system: your group and personal values. Discover them and you will know why you do what you do—which, in the end, is often more important than just doing.

If you do not feel that you have complete freedom, what are the social forces or values that limit your options? Put another way, what is preventing you from taking a trip around the world, like some people your age do, just working odd jobs, or what has kept you on your course through grade school, high school, and now college—unlike most of the people your age in the world?

[1] Adapted by permission from training materials used by Richard B. Lawhon, Faculty Training Workshop, The Freshman Year Experience, University of South Carolina.

Group Activity 12.2 *Comparing Your Values*

Purpose: Although introspection is a good place to start examining and discovering your values, remember that familiar things are sometimes hard to see. You have been pickled and marinated in a cultural view, a value blend of points of view based on particular survival needs—some real, some not so real. You assume that the options you see are reality, when, in fact, most of what you see is distorted by the values and assumptions you give to your social and physical world.

In this activity you will begin with your responses and reflections in Exercise 12.1 and examine the similarities and differences between your values and those of your classmates.

Directions: Form small groups of no more than five students and no less than three. Compare your responses to the statements and questions in Exercise 12.1. Note three places in which members of your group differ strongly. Discuss your differences to investigate the origin of your contrasting values (family, tradition, experience) and how your actions and the consequences of your actions differ in your lives because of your values. For example, one person may value money while another person may value knowledge—both may study hard, learn different things, and have different outcomes in terms of careers and happiness. The point is to help you understand how each person uses values to guide his or her actions to solve a problem. You may have a common problem and approach it with different values and actions; note this.

During your discussion, have one member of your group record three significant contrasts in problems, values, actions, and outcomes. Report to the class after the discussion process is concluded.

Closure: Values are hard to get a handle on at first. But part of being a citizen in a democracy is understanding the guidance system that moves you and others in one direction or another. Begin with introspection, proceed with discussion, and keep looking. The hidden world of values will become more and more apparent to you as you exercise your new lenses.

Group Activity 12.3 *Personal Goals Auction*[2]

Purpose: Making choices between one value (action) and another is the constant challenge of a free person, as Richard Morrill observed in *College Is Only the Beginning*. This activity is designed to force you to establish some priorities for yourself while getting a view of the priorities of your peers.

Directions: Each member of your class has $100,000 to bid for values in your class auction. Review the following list of life goals, which will be auctioned off in your class. Decide which values you want and how much you are willing to bid to obtain them. Bid in increments of $1,000. Only the highest bid will achieve the life goal.

   After a careful review of the goals, distribute your money according to your priorities in the first column of the Budget Bidding Record 12.3A, which follows the goals description.

   Your instructor will auction off the life goals in a random order. If you are forced of overbid your budget to obtain a goal, you must adjust the amount you can bid on another goal. *Do not exceed $100,000.*

   After each bidding, whether you win the goal or not, record the amount you bid and the sale price on the Budget Bidding Record 12.3A.

Personal Life Goals Description

An Exciting Life: You will lead an exciting, stimulating life, encountering a wide range of new experiences with the confidence that you are equal to all challenges and able to enjoy whatever comes your way.

Financial Security: You will have sufficient money to support any material needs or desires you have, plus enough surplus wealth to use for any purpose of your choice, be it pampering others, contributing to charity, or assuring social status.

Personal Freedom: You will have a life of independence, always being able to do what you know is right for *you* in the here-and-now, without any interference from others.

Pleasure: You will lead an enjoyable, leisurely life. You will not be rushed by commitments, and all possible pleasures will be

[2]Adapted by permission from training materials used by Richard B. Lawhon, Faculty Training Workshop, The Freshman Year Experience, University of South Carolina.

readily available.

Closeness to God: You will experience a communication with God, Who will know that you are serving Him/Her, and you will achieve His/Her purpose for you.

A World of Beauty: You will live close to the beauty of nature and to the beauty of fine art, literature, music, and the theater.

Job Satisfaction: You will be recognized by all as being the best in your profession, contributing more than you ever hoped and achieving everything you ever dreamed.

Long Life and Good Health: You will live far longer than the normal life expectancy, and your physical and mental health will be superb. You will benefit from both the vitality of youthfulness and wisdom born of experience.

A Comprehensive Personal Library: You will possess a personal library containing every bit of information ever recorded. The information will be totally accessible—you will be able to receive immediately any item you request, in printed or voice-recorded form.

An Ideal Setting: You will have a house overlooking the most beautiful scenery in the world. The house will have all the atmosphere, space, and facilities necessary to provide you and others of your choice with a perfect environment.

A Perfect Love Affair: You will experience an emotional and sexual relationship with a person of great physical and emotional attractiveness—a person who will have the same expectations of the affair as you. You will have absolute control over who is aware of the affair.

Universal Harmony: You will live in a world in which equal opportunity for all and the love of humanity are recognized as the primary value.

A Perfect Family Life: You and your family will experience ideal relationships together, each finding the needed love and security to assure personal growth within the family unit.

Inner Peace: You will be free from all inner conflicts, secure in the knowledge that you will always make right decisions and continue effective personal functioning.

Intelligence: You will function at full mental capacity, being able to perceive solutions to critical problems and to understand logical relationships between ideas.

Political Power: You will be in a position to control the destinies of most people in the civilized world. You will have absolute power to institute any program or policy you choose and will be able to gain the cooperation of any person or organization required by your purpose.

An Authentic World: You will live in a world in which all people are open, honest, and totally able to relate authentically with one another. Whatever feelings exist will be openly shared.

Fame: You will receive the respect and admiration of all and will be in demand at prominent social occasions and decision-making conferences.

Social Service: You will have the opportunity, the skill, and the resources to serve the sick and needy of the world. Full effort on your part will eliminate sickness and need in your lifetime.

Creativity: You will be able to formulate innovative ways of communicating perceptive understanding. You will have unusually fine command of several art media, as well as verbal creativity.

Self-Esteem: You will respect yourself, knowing that you are realizing your potential and that you are a person of great worth.

Deep Friendships: You will have many close and meaningful relationships with people you would choose to know well.

Mature Love: You will attain lasting spiritual and sexual intimacy with another.

Wisdom: You will have a mature understanding of life and will be sought out by others to furnish advice and counsel.

Closure: This activity placed you in competition with your peers for life goals that in fact represent values that guide people's lives. It forced you to make decisions; you had to weigh one value against another. In the end, you had to decide what was important to you as opposed to what was important to your peers.

Budget Bidding Record 12.3A

Item	Amount Budgeted	Amount Bid	Sale Price
An exciting life			
Financial security			
Personal freedom			
Pleasure			
Closeness to God			
A world of beauty			
Job satisfaction			
A long life			
Personal library			
An ideal setting			
A perfect love affair			
Universal harmony			
Perfect family life			
Inner peace			
Intelligence			
Political power			
An authentic world			
Fame			
Social service			
Creativity			
Self-esteem			
Deep friendships			
Mature love			
Wisdom			

Your top 3 life goal choices:	The top 3 goals you won:	The top 3 goals as indicated by bids:	Biggest surprise to you:
1.	1.	1.	1.
2.	2.	2.	2.
3.	3.	3.	3.

Group Activity 12.4 *The Social Problem*[3]

Purpose: The purpose of this activity is to present you with a problem that requires you to discuss a value judgment with several of your classmates. This is typical of the kinds of social problems that the liberal arts prepare us to confront. **Note:** The presentation of this problem does not imply that I personally agree with the actions taken by the characters in this scenario. However, the sad fact is that the shift in sexual morality in some regions combined with a poor understanding of conception or contraception have resulted in many unwanted pregnancies and abortion. This exercise is presented in the hope that our freshmen will apply their morals and values to the situation and better understand the consequences of their actions.

Directions: Read the scenario that follows. Number the characters listed according to their responsibility for Susan's death. Identify the least responsible as #8 and the most responsible as #1. Then form small groups of five students and attempt to arrive at an agreement on the order of responsibility.

After discussing responsibility, try defining: **(1)** the problem represented in this scenario; **(2)** the two main causes of the problem; and **(3)** a recommendation for preventing a recurrence of the problem. Summarize the results of your discussions for the other members of your freshman seminar.

The Scenario

Susan came from a small town where her widowed father was a minister. He raised her very strictly, and it was only with great reluctance that he allowed her to go away to college. He feared that the big city would corrupt her. As she boarded the bus, he warned her, "If I ever find out that you've been fooling around with boys or using alcohol or drugs, I'll cut you off from all financial support and never let you enter our home again."

Susan had always obeyed her father and intended to do so while at college. She did stay away from drugs and alcohol; however, in October she began dating Larry, a fellow student in her religion class. By December they were sleeping together. And when she returned from Christmas vacation, she discovered that she was pregnant. Neither her father, the private church-affiliated schools, nor the college they attended had ever mentioned birth control. Susan and Larry had not taken the proper precautions when sleeping together.

Larry did not want to get married, and Susan knew that when her father came to take her home in May the pregnancy would be obvious. Panic-stricken, she decided to have an abortion. She went to one of the agencies that advertised help for unwanted pregnancies in the school newspaper. At the agency she learned that an abortion would cost her $500. Knowing that she could not earn this sum in time, she asked Larry for a loan. "I'm sorry, but I don't have that kind of money," he replied. "Besides, you should have been more careful."

Then she asked her best friend Allison for the money. "I don't approve of abortion." she said. "I can't lend you money to destroy life."

In desperation, Susan approached one of the dorm custodians, who was rumored to be a former prostitute. "Sure. I've got a concoction that will make you miscarry—no charge," said the woman.

After taking the mixture, Susan did miscarry, but in the process she hemorrhaged severely and died.

Responsibility Rating for Characters

Susan _____   Agency head _____

Susan's father _____   Allison _____

Larry _____   The custodian _____

The private church-affiliated schools _____

Susan's college_____

Closure: When situations like this occur in life, the questions of right and wrong go round and round. At some point you must decide how your values, morals, and responsibility relate to larger social problems. As a final moment of reflection for yourself, consider which liberal arts courses might have been helpful for the characters in the scenario.

Journal Entry

List your three highest values from Group Activity 12.3. Discuss whether these values are short-term or lifelong, whether they are physical (material wealth) or spiritual (emotional/nonmaterial), and the limit (highest level) to the satisfaction you can obtain in your life by following these values.

❖ Chapter 13 ❖

Relationships
Building Bridges to Others

Our world is built on relationships. We each have different relationships with ourselves, our environment, parents, siblings,
friends, neighbors, roommates, lovers, faculty, and of course—
the largest category of all—strangers. For most of us, the
relationships we have with ourselves and significant others[1]
determine the way we act toward the people and things that
are personally unknown to us.

I was very pleased to be invited to contribute a chapter on
relationships to the 1989 edition of *College Is Only the Beginning*, and of course to include a chapter on the subject in this
book as well. When I train faculty to teach freshmen seminars,
or new student seminars as we call them at Duquesne University, I begin with relationships. Until most freshmen establish
meaningful relationships, little else happens for them.

---

[1]"Significant other" refers to those people we take as role models. Most often
our significant others are older members of our family. For an in-depth discussion of
how the individual emerges into society beginning with the "I" and "me" perspective, developing through contact with significant others and finally acquiring
the "generalized other" perspective, see George Herbert Mead, *Mind, Self and
Society* (Chicago: University of Chicago Press, 1934).

When you arrived on your college campus, your focus, apart from your bureaucratic mission, was on relationships. If you were like most freshmen, you watched others making friends and tried to make new friends for yourself. Whether you thought about it or not, you tended to select people to meet according to what you were looking for in a relationship. And you did not or will not feel comfortable or at home on your college campus until you build some significant relationships.

The exercises in this chapter will help you define the relationships that you want, as well as the values that you would prefer to have guiding the interaction in your relationships. This is the time when you begin to form more adult relationships that will last the rest of your life. It's worth taking a little time to start out right.

Individual Exercise 13.1 *Starting at the Foundation*

Purpose: Most of your relating behaviors and instincts developed through interaction between you and those around you at a young age. For most people, the family system of relating is the initial, if not most significant, influence on their relating behavior. Until you reflect on why you do what you do, and why you react to certain situations in predictable ways, you will be swept through relationships rather than be a creator of them. This exercise and following activities will help you sharpen your awareness of your communication strategies in relationships. Then you can begin to create the kinds of relationships that are most fulfilling and beneficial to you and others.

Directions: The following series of questions begins with your origin in your family or group and extends to your relationship with your environment. Although some of these questions could take pages to respond to, for the purpose of this exercise, please outline your answer briefly. (Your right to privacy ensures that you do not have to share this information with anyone, but it is good to spell it out for yourself.)

1. Who raised you?

_____

2. What size family or group did you grow up in?

_____

3. Were emotions expressed openly in your group or family?

_____

_____

_____

4. Did your family or group members assert themselves openly to each other or did they talk through third parties? Give an example.

_____

_____

_____

5. Do you express your feelings and needs openly, through a third party, or hope that others will guess your feelings and needs? Give an example.

_____

_____

_____

6. Did your family or group stay together or break up? What effect did this have on you?

_____

_____

_____

7. Did you live in the same place, move around the same area, move far away from your first friends, move often? What effect did your moving or staying have on the way you look at relationships? Give an example.

_____

_____

_____

8. Name three things that you like about your best friend:

a. _____

b. _____

c. _____

9. What other qualities would you like to have in a friend?

_____

_____

_____

10. What three things would occur on an ideal first date?

a. _____

b. _____

c. _____

11. Would you tell your date what you hope will occur? Why or why not?

_____

_____

_____

12. Would you ask your date what he or she hopes will occur? Why or why not?

_____

_____

_____

13. Imagine that you could hate a group of people. Give five reasons someone should hate them:

a. _____

b. _____

c. _____

d. _____

e. _____

14. Imagine that you could like a group of people. Give five reasons someone should like them:

a. _____

b. _____

c. _____

d. _____

e. _____

15. Do you like nature? What is your relationship with nature?

_____

_____

_____

16. What is the relationship between your existence and nature?

_____

_____

_____

17. How does your relationship with nature help preserve nature?

_____

_____

_____

18. How does your relationship with nature help destroy nature?

_____

_____

_____

19. Will the earth be better or worse because of your existence on it?

_____

_____

_____

Closure: These questions were designed to help you discover some of your starting points or values that guide you in different relationships. In some ways these starting points are like lenses through which you view special others, groups of others, or your physical environment. If you grew up in a family in which adults showed affection by giving gifts, you would probably respond to touching differently than would someone who grew up in a family whose members hugged often. Similarly, if your ideal first date includes physical closeness, you may not fare well with someone who likes to keep a comfortable distance until he or she can build trust. It is important to know your preferences and to know _why_ you prefer one thing over another.

Group Activity 13.2 *Starting on the Interpersonal Level*

Purpose: We meet people, make assumptions about them, and decide on first impressions whether we like them or not. We give off nonverbal signals, read nonverbal signals, yet our same signals do not always mean the same thing. This exercise is designed to help you record your observations in an interpersonal situation, so that you can get a sense of how well you listen to *everything* that is being communicated between you and the other person.

Directions: For 20 minutes talk to a person in the class you have not previously known, on any subject (except the questionnaire in this activity). Then, either by guess or actual data that came out, fill out the following form on the other person.[2] *Don't review the following form until after your discussion!*

1. His (her) age _____.

2. He (she) is one of _____ children.

3. He (she) is _____ in the order of siblings.

4. He (she) comes from a community of _____ (number of) people.

5. He (she) is closer to his (her) father, mother. (*circle one*)

6. His (her) father had _____ years of education.

7. His (her) mother had _____ years of education.

8. His (her) political sympathies lie with the _____ party.

9. He (she) is a liberal, conservative, reactionary in social issues. (*circle one*)

(*circle one number below*)

10. He (she) is relaxed   1 2 3 4 5 6 7   tense in social situations.

11. He (she) is usually moody   1 2 3 4 5 6 7   cheerful.

12. He (she) is emotionally stable   1 2 3 4 5 6 7   unstable.

13. He (she) is athletically inclined   1 2 3 4 5 6 7   not inclined.

---

[2]Adapted from Charles T. Brown and Paul W. Keller, *Monologue to Dialogue: An Exploration of Interpersonal Communication*, 2nd ed., ©1979, pp.80–81. Adapted by permission of Prentice-Hall, Inc., Englewood Cliffs, New Jersey.

14. He (she) is interested in: (*circle one number below*)

Athletics	very much	1 2 3 4 5 6 7	not much
Art	very much	1 2 3 4 5 6 7	not much
Music	very much	1 2 3 4 5 6 7	not much
Drama	very much	1 2 3 4 5 6 7	not much
Philosophy	very much	1 2 3 4 5 6 7	not much
Science	very much	1 2 3 4 5 6 7	not much
Mathematics	very much	1 2 3 4 5 6 7	not much
Religion	very much	1 2 3 4 5 6 7	not much
Travel	very much	1 2 3 4 5 6 7	not much
People	very much	1 2 3 4 5 6 7	not much
Our conversation	very much	1 2 3 4 5 6 7	not much

Having filled out this form, now have the other person correct it. From your own correction of the other person's awareness of you, what did you learn? How revealing are you? How hard are you to read? Few corrections usually indicate that a person with strong nonverbal signals and open style communicated to a perceptive listener.

Closure: This exercise should have given you some insight into the effectiveness of the communication style that you use in one-to-one communication. You can make proper decisions about your relationships only if you are receiving correct information about the other person. If you had a lot of corrections made to your form about your observations, it could be a signal to you to improve your communication skills on the interpersonal level. For some practice in that area, try Group Activity 13.3.

Group Activity 13.3 *Listening to Others in Addition to Ourselves*

Purpose: In our society men often interrupt women in conversation. Interruption is a sign of dominance, because the interrupted one does not get a chance to speak. Of course, interruption does not improve communication or the situation of either party. The interrupted person is often frustrated, and the interrupter often lacks vital information on which to base decisions. Maintaining a relationship in which one person interrupts another is difficult at best. This activity is designed to heighten your awareness of the most critical factor in relationships: *listening*.

Directions, Part 1: Form groups of four, preferably of mixed gender. Everyone should write down five statements about himself or herself and five questions about something that he or she would really like to know. Within each group count off: 1-2-1-2. Going around the group, 1 reads a question 2 interrupts on the third word by forcefully reading a statement. Continuing, the other 1 reads a question, the other 2 interrupts on the third word by forcefully reading a statement. After the 1's have finished all their questions and have been interrupted every time by a 2, the 2's should start with their questions and be similarly interrupted by the 1's statements.

Directions, Part 2: After all have been interrupted, discuss for five minutes how you felt when you were interrupted and how you felt interrupting the other.

Directions, Part 3: After that brief discussion, each group member asks one of his or her questions and the members of the group listen and respond briefly.

Conclusion: After questions and a brief discussion, each member of the group should tell the other three what he or she learned about them from listening and responding to their questions.

Closure: The next time you are in a conversation, attend to whether you interrupt others or others interrupt you. If you catch yourself interrupting, excuse yourself and ask the other person to continue. If you are interrupted, you can regain the right to speak by saying "Excuse me, I was speaking." If that phrase does not bring forth the appropriate response, forget it; no one is listening anyway.

Group Activity 13.4 *Knowing Strangers*

Purpose: Although one out of every seven people that you meet will know someone that you know, the world still appears to be populated by strangers. When we don't know people well, we tend to assume things about them. The more they are culturally or physically different from us, or the more they are in conflict with us, the more likely we are to ascribe negative stereotypes to them.

Without the facts about a people, we will base our relationship with them on these stereotypes—which only produces more misunderstanding and distrust. Stereotypes are generalizations about other people which are usually not true but are often accepted as fact. The purpose of this activity is to heighten your awareness of the negative impact that stereotypes can have in our decision making and on peace in the world.

Note: I participated in this activity as it was directed by a young Israeli woman at the Society for Intercultural Education Training and Research Annual Conference in 1985 in Washington, D.C. At that time she used Jews and Arabs as the contrast ethnic people in the training activity, which was used in the Mideast to promote understanding and peace.

Directions: As a class, select two ethnic groups that are known to the students in the class. Local ethnic groups are usually recommended for this exercise. Form four groups. Group 1 must make a list of all the positive attributes they have ever heard about Ethnic People A. Group 2 must make a list of all the negative attributes they have ever heard about Ethnic People A. Group 3 must make a list of all the positive attributes they have ever heard about Ethnic People B. Group 4 must make a list of all the negative attributes they have ever heard about Ethnic People B.

When the four groups have finished their lists, the lists should be written on the chalkboard or large sheets of paper so all can see. The class should then respond to the following questions in discussion:

1. What is the similarity between the attribute lists for the A's and the B's?
2. Would you trust anybody with such negative attributes?
3. Would you trust anybody with such positive attributes?
4. Do any of the lists depict an accurate picture of a people?
5. Give examples of how you would act toward someone if you believed that the negative list of attributes was an accurate description of him or her.
6. Give an example from American history in which negative stereotypes directed social policy.
7. Give two examples from recent events that illustrate the use of negative stereotypes guiding social action.

Group Activity 13.5 *Your Relationship with the Earth*

Purpose: For the first time in the history of *Homo erectus*, we have the power to alter the earth according to our desires. Our heavy industry, our military, our agriculture—literally our way of life—attempt to control nature. The most commonly used strategy of control is to reduce or wipe out the complexity of nature (for example, the rain forests or herbicides in USA) and then produce mass quantities of one crop. The weakness of this method is that a single virus can wipe out a simplified system of this kind overnight, but usually one virus cannot destroy a complex system.

In modern times, our culture has set in motion a social system that is negatively affecting the quality of our drinking water, the ozone layer that protects us from solar radiation, the acidity of rain now burning out our forests, lakes, and streams, the number of species that exist on earth—and the list goes on. The purpose of this activity is to help freshmen gain an awareness of the environmental challenges facing their generation and the values that led us to create these potential ecological disasters.

Directions: Form groups of no less than three and no more than five. Each group should elect to focus on one of these environmental problems:

1. *Land and soil:* erosion, irrigation, herbicides, toxic waste
2. *Water:* lakes, streams, drinking water, acid rain, toxic waste
3. *Air:* industrial pollution, ozone layer, acid rain
4. *Plants and trees:* maintenance, cultivation, and destruction
5. *Animals:* destruction of habitat, rapid extension of species

Students should feel free to shift groups during the beginning of this activity if another group has elected an approach that is more interesting to the individual. After the group chooses an environmental area, each group member should follow the Individual Research Guide.

Individual Research Guide

Pick three of the media resource areas listed on the following page. Each resource area should be covered by at least one member of your group. Review one item in each selected medium that offers information on your group topic. Take notes and report back to your group on what you found.

Video or film:	documentary, PBS report
Book:	there are hundreds of books for the non-technical reader
Magazine article:	at least three pages long
Interview:	contact your local conservation groups, such as Audubon, Sierra Club, forestry representative
Government:	EPA reports and other publications
Newspaper:	*New York Times, Wall Street Journal* or *Christian Science Monitor* often have in-depth coverage.

Each individual should fill out the Individual Research Report Form 13.5A, make a copy for the members of his or her group, and orally summarize to the group. After all individual reports are in, the group report should be outlined with a bibliography and the Group Research Report Form 13.5B used as the first page summary.

Each group should be careful to distill the information that they gathered and to take a hard look at the values that are guiding our relationship with the earth.

Final oral report: With the class sitting in a circle and each group still seated together, a spokesperson from each group should summarize the group's findings and conclusions (20–30 minutes). The spokesperson should call on individuals in his or her group for clarification on specific details. The best reports could be submitted to campus or regional publications or media.

Closure: This activity should have given you a good understanding of the problems we are facing today and the values that guide our relationship with the earth. If we are going to pass on a living planet to the next generation, we must start working on this relationship.

Journal Entry

Write several paragraphs on this question: What is the relationship between the values that guide your relationship with yourself and close friends/family members and the values that guide your relationship with the earth?

Individual Research Report Form 13.5A

Source and Citation	Example of the Problem	Causes of the Problem

Group Research Report Form 13.5B

Causes of the Problem	Values Behind the Causes	Solutions to the Problem	
		Long term	**Short term**
Conclusion:	Conclusion:	Conclusion:	Conclusion:

❖ Chapter 14 ❖

Leadership and Success
Getting Results

When I look back on my high school days, I think: "Oh, what a lost puppy you were." I could not have found my way out of a paper bag, let alone take charge of a group and get results. Yet four years after I graduated from the 12th grade, I was leaving college with a B.A., a place in *Who's Who Among Students in American Colleges and Universities 1970,* and a successful student career that included making reforms in student government, creating a student welfare committee, and holding 17 offices, including dorm council member, secretary of interfraternity council, and chairman of a college-wide committee that guided the design of our student union.

What happened to the lost puppy? Did he magically change into one of those dynamic student leaders he stood in awe of in high school? I think the lost puppy in me just got lucky. My room was beside that of the resident assistant, who belonged to the fraternity that controlled student government. We became friends. I became a fraternity brother and was strongly encouraged to join student government. With the support of my new friends, the fraternity brothers, I became a student government representative. In that role I found out that if I took on a task that everyone wanted done, I was praised. If I accomplished the task, I was allowed to take on greater tasks.

I will always believe that my road to success started in that freshman experience when I was at the right place at the right time—and took full advantage of it. You can just as easily put yourself in the right place by offering yourself as an open, honest, friendly person to upperclassmen who know their way around and can get you involved. Getting into the existing network or system is the key to getting started.

As Dennis Pruitt observed in *College Is Only the Beginning* (1985), there are four things college leadership can teach you that will help you to succeed later in life: **(1)** Learn to select the right activity for the right audience. **(2)** Learn to promote your activity. **(3)** Learn to actually produce an activity—for example, pull a team together and get everyone to perform assigned tasks. **(4)** Learn to evaluate the success of the event so that you can improve on it next time. As long as there is a problem to solve or a need unfilled, there is room for one more leader. And once you learn the skills of leadership, you will gain the respect of others and control over your future. Give it a try!

Note: I do not want to imply that you are a lost puppy if you are not a joiner. Joining and participating in college groups can prepare you for some careers; indeed, most occupations require some kind of group work. However, some people work better alone. Although some of their career activities require group contact, artists, laboratory scientists, and accountants often must work alone. Ultimately you must decide for yourself if learning to work in groups or being a leader is important to you. If you enjoy yourself in solitude, don't be intimidated into joining or trying to be a leader. Be yourself.

Group Activity 14.1 *Discussion on Group Leadership Attitudes*

Purpose: Leadership requires a knowledge of group process. There are ways of working with a group to get things done and ways of working against a group to make things fall apart. This exercise is designed to heighten your awareness of some successful group–process strategies. Remember two things: In our culture a group must come to consensus before the members can work together, and consensus must never be gained at the loss of individual motivation.

Directions: This activity consists of two questions followed by eight attitude statements. Think about how you would answer the following two questions as they apply to the eight attitude statements. Then the entire class should discuss each student's answers until the class arrives at consensus. You will find it easier to discuss the questions if you use concrete examples whenever possible.

Questions

❖   What effect would the following attitude statements have on long-term group consensus?
❖   What effect would the following attitude statements have on the motivation of each member?

Attitude Statements

1. It is best to get to know all the members of the group socially before you try to work with them.
2. Individual assignments or committee assignments should be made by the leader without regard to the interests of each group member.
3. If you think the group is wrong, you should act on your own, regardless of what other members have voted to do.
4. Opinions should be expressed in meetings only when the leader asks for feedback.
5. The best leaders are usually experts in everything—which is how they know what is the best thing to do.
6. If the assignments of the group members are made according to their interests, they will be motivated to complete the task.
7. When the group leader is working to his or her capacity, he or she should not be openly criticized even if he or she is doing something wrong.
8. When a group member makes a serious mistake, the situation should be discussed in front of everyone at a meeting.

Closure: Group process is not an exact science. The best way to get started is to sharpen your intuition with discussions about group process and then proceed with some small group–process exercises like Activity 14.2.

Group Activity 14.2 *Exploring Leadership Principles*

Purpose: In general, Europeans are comfortable carrying on a conversation on the level of general principles and theory, whereas Americans, with our empirical view of the world, prefer an example to clarify the principle. This activity is designed to aid students in fixing leadership principles in their minds by having them attach their own examples to the principles.

Directions: Form groups of no more than five. Each group must review the following leadership principles with each group member contributing examples of the principles from his or her own life observations. One member of each group should record what the group agrees is the best example of each principle. After all groups have listed their examples, the class at large should discuss the principles and examples in order to determine which example best illustrates the principle.

Leadership Principles

1. Leadership and power are often confused. A good leader is first of all a good servant. The power of a leader comes from the group's recognition of past service.
2. A good leader listens to the needs of the members, taps the skills of the members, and encourages individual members to apply their stronger skills to meet individual and group needs.
3. A good leader increases the communication between group members, thus enhancing the bond that holds the group together.
4. A good leader reviews the objectives of the group with the members in order to determine whether the members are in agreement on all levels.
5. A good leader observes the natural friendships among certain group members and recognizes these bonds as resources for building motivation and cooperation.
6. A good leader recognizes the natural personality conflicts within a group and is careful to keep communication open, honest, fair, and nondivisive.

7. A good leader recognizes the factions within the group and is careful to give each faction tasks that its constituents can accomplish with pride.
8. A good leader tries to avoid involvement in personality conflicts, in order to render fair and objective judgments when the need arises.
9. A good leader cares about the well-being of all, demonstrating this by asking about the situations that are important to the others.
10. A good leader is always mindful of the public image of the group and tries to guide each and all so that the larger community will support and perpetuate the existence of the group.

Closure: This activity gives you some direction about what a group leader has to do on an interpersonal level. Don't confuse yourself by thinking that the business on the agenda is the focus of the leader's attention. The interpersonal aspects take much more energy than other matters. And when the relationships in a group are working, all else falls into place.

Group Activity 14.3 *Developing a Group*

Purpose: There are many college groups already established that freshmen can join. Most students see their options limited to the choice of joining the existing groups or remaining "independent." The reason students assume this perspective is that there is rarely a mechanism for them to organize themselves according to their own interests or concerns. Freshmen are totally unorganized as a group. They are unaware of the problems of the campus and are usually intimidated by the size and complexity of the social structure they have entered.

This activity is designed to help freshmen **(1)** discover the problems and needs of their campus society; **(2)** define their personal interests and skills as they relate to interests and skills of their peers; and **(3)** develop a viable organization that will address the campus problems and needs while building on their interests and skills.

One group in my class last term decided that they would like to develop a peer counseling team on campus. They met with administrators in charge of counseling services, studied the role played by peer counselors, made a presentation on the need for their idea, and passed around a sign-up sheet for other students who would like to be trained as peer counselors. At this point we now have more than 20 students who are ready to work with us.

Directions, Part 1: (*20-minute process*) Form groups of five. Continue the groups from Activity 14.2, if possible. Each group should elect a discussion leader and a recorder who can take good notes. Each group member should be assigned to interview one upperclassman from a recognized group on campus and one who is "independent." The purpose of the interview is to discover the history of campus problems and previous attempts at solving these problems. (A problem can be what to do on the weekend for entertainment, as well as more serious issues like health, drugs, and alcohol—which are sometimes associated with having nothing to do.) One of the group members should locate some old editions of the campus newspaper in the library and review the news and editorials that relate to campus problems.

Determine who will go where, to find what, and when the group members will meet again to share their findings. Figure about a week for fact finding.

Directions, Part 2: (*one class period about a week later*) The leader will first read one of the following statements, complete it, and then ask the other group members to repeat the statement and complete it. Everyone has the right to pass.

1. One need this group could serve is . . .
2. The skills I could offer to this group are . . .
3. One thing that makes me happy is . . .
4. I get excited when . . .
5. I feel comfortable when . . .
6. Something I'd like to change about myself is . . .
7. The one thing I demand of others is . . .
8. The objective (problem solution) this group should try for is . . .
9. The qualities our members need to meet the objective are . . .

Send a memo to your class instructor defining objectives that your group is considering and what qualities the members of your group could bring to the task. Note: Developing a new group does not limit your chances of joining an existing group now or later. I very often develop new ideas with a new small group and later bring the growing projects into larger existing groups (who are often less likely to take on new, untried ideas).

Closure: This activity should have showed you how different personalities come together to make up a viable group. Accept the differences and build on them.

Group Activity 14.4 *Building a Campus Group*

Purpose: Some members of the class may want to continue the development of their group. The purpose of this activity is to build on the enthusiasm of class participants for developing a more responsive campus society. If some class members do not wish to continue with the group building, that is fine. They could serve as advisers, join other groups, or even sit in a circle around a working group and later be given an opportunity to make observations about which group dynamics seem to have a positive impact on the group project development process.

Directions: Keeping in mind your recent responses to the statements in Activity 14.3, write an advertisement or design a presentation that will attract new members to your group. You may want to develop both approaches. However, consider the talents of your present members and take on a task that they can accomplish in a short amount of time.

You should also decide how many new members you can bring in at one time and still maintain the identity of the group. After all ads are written they should be circulated around the class for feedback. Presentations should be rehearsed and presented to the class for feedback. The final draft of ads should be posted and/or placed in campus newspapers. Presentations should be performed in front of audiences likely to contain potential members, or videotaped and shown to small groups or aired over campus TV stations.

Closure: It is easy to get a new group started or to get involved with an existing group. Everything in the social world happens one step at a time. Take the first step and you won't regret it.

Journal Entry

Discuss your leadership strengths and weaknesses. How would you like improve your skills by applying them in your social environment? Define a realistic objective for applying and strengthening your skills this year.

❖ Chapter 15 ❖

Your College Residence

Ideally, when you selected a college you did so because that institution met the academic, economic, and social needs and goals you had defined for yourself. Your college residence will have almost as much impact on your ability to meet your needs and goals as your regular attendance to class.

The traditional freshman residence hall is filled with young people who have not been away from home for extended periods of time. The initial celebration of freedom can go on for months. If you are a resident, you should be concerned that your new environment could turn into a zoo if you and your neighbors do not define what you want and organize yourselves to get it.

Your style of interpersonal and nonverbal communication will greatly affect your relationship with your roommate(s). You cannot expect your roommate(s) to conform to your lifestyle and values. You come from different families, with different strategies for problem solving. In the early stage of your relationship with your roommate(s) you should establish some ground rules and communication channels to ensure a com-

149

fortable and supportive environment for academic success.

If you have elected to commute to college, you should be careful to recognize the impact that college will have on your life, as compared to the impact of high school. You will not have the free time that you had during high school. Between the increase in study and research, commuting, and perhaps employment because of added expenses, the amount of time you will have for family involvement and chores should be examined and renegotiated early in your first term.

Individual Exercise 15.1 *Defining Your Position*

Residents

Purpose: Too often roommates have disagreements because they have not thought out the implications of sharing space with each other. This exercise will help you and your roommate(s) define your expectations and your values in action so that both of you can come to an agreement before a conflict arises.

Directions: On a separate sheet of paper write your response to the following:

1. Have you ever shared a room with another person? If yes, what did you like and dislike about the situation? If no, how prepared do you think you are to share your space?
2. How do you feel about other people using your things? If you don't mind some borrowing, what prior arrangements should be made?
3. What are your preferences for neatness? When should a room be cleaned?
4. What are your preferences for quiet? Can you study with the TV on, music playing, or people talking?
5. How do you feel about having guests in during the day or overnight? What is the responsibility of the roommate(s) who is (are) having the guest? How would you feel if your roommate(s) had a guest of the opposite sex in your room while you were trying to sleep?
6. How many hours of sleep do you need each night? What hours do you prefer to sleep?

7. What temperature do you like your room? Do you prefer to have the windows open or closed?

8. Should smoking be permitted in your room?

9. How should jointly owned or used objects be paid for, such as TV and phone,?

10. Should alcohol or drugs be permitted in your room?

11. How would you like to arrange and decorate your room(s)?

12. Is it important for you to get messages? If yes, what arrangements should be made with your roommate(s)?

After you have defined your position on these matters, compare your responses with those of your roommate(s). Determine which responses are similar, which are close, and which represent very different points of view. Discuss the differences, observing the guidelines in "Communication/Negotiation Tips" following the commuter directions.

Commuters

Purpose: Commuters often assume that home life will remain the same as in high school days. Too often the impact of the increased academic load and personal involvement of the college experience causes conflict with families and old friends. This exercise will help you establish a new agenda with those you live with.

Directions: On a separate sheet of paper write your response to the following:

1. Are there chores and responsibilities you would like to rearrange or renegotiate with parents, siblings, spouse, or children?

2. How will your time needs differ from previous years?

3. Is your present study area going to be adequate for the additional work you will be required to do in college?

4. How will you get involved in campus life? Do you plan to join activities, meet residents, and so on?

5. Will you need a place to study between classes?

6. Do you have problems with parking, child care, transportation?

7. What other problems or issues are important to you in your new situation?

8. Are you getting the kind of emotional support from your family that you need?

Discuss these concerns with your family or commuter affairs officer, observing the guidelines that follow.

Communication/Negotiation Tips

❖ Use only neutral language when you are discussing personal issues. An example of neutral language: "When you bring in visitors while I am studying I get annoyed." Examples of confrontational language are: "You are inconsiderate when you bring in visitors." or "When you do (x) you make me mad."

❖ Be prepared before you start to negotiate. Know what you want, what you will accept, and what you will not tolerate, so that when you are listening to your roommate(s) or family you will have a system for evaluating the contract proposals.

❖ In any negotiation situation, start with the easiest issues to resolve so that you can form a bond of agreement. Just imagine how alienated everyone would feel if the first issue discussed resulted in a major disagreement.

❖ When negotiation starts, each participant should be given a chance to speak without disruption. The others should be engaged in active listening—perhaps even making notes about where they agree and disagree.

❖ In order to aid calm, friendship-building negotiation, the process should go on at a predetermined time, in a shared part of your environment, with as little distraction as possible. Quiet music supports a calm, thoughtful process. The best nonverbal position to take is a relaxed posture. Sit facing each other at a comfortable distance.

❖ All discussions should be kept confidential. You cannot build a relationship in a fishbowl. In the future there may be personal things you will want to share. Trust and confidentiality will allow the sharing to happen.

Individual Exercise 15.2   *Contract Negotiation*

Purpose: Written contracts are important. People tend to reshape their memory to accommodate new circumstances. Also, written contracts bring people together in an act of defining their relationship clearly and carefully. The purpose of this exercise is to create a more open understanding between you and those you must interact with during your freshman year.

Resident Directions: Following the communication tips, begin with the items on which you and your roommate(s) hold similar positions. Write a contract that establishes ground rules for your shared and private space. After completing the easiest category of issues, proceed in calm negotiation until you have arrived at a contract that both of you can live with. Review the contract every several weeks and openly discuss any infractions in neutral language.

Commuter Directions: Follow the same negotiation procedures as in resident directions with those who have the most effect on your environment. Sometimes parents, siblings, spouse, children, or even neighbors may need to be involved in this process.

Closure: If you took your time and proceeded with respect for the others in your life, you should have developed a clear set of operating rules for your living environment. Remember, a contract can always be renegotiated—but you must have one to start with first.

Group Activity 15.3 *Reviewing Negotiations*

Purpose: All new skills take time to learn. Some of you will be better negotiators than others. If you find yourself reluctant to bring up certain points, you might want to look at the chapters on assertiveness in this book as well as in *College Is Only the Beginning*. This exercise will give you a chance to see how others negotiate, what problems they encountered, and how they resolved them.

Directions: Have the members of the class decide which part of the negotiation process in Exercises 15.1 and 15.2 was most interesting to them. The class participants should be prepared to discuss the most interesting issue. Whenever confidentiality is a concern, permission to discuss the issues should be requested from your negotiation partners.

Closure: Like any other skill, negotiation takes time to learn. By now you should have an idea of how to proceed in a negotiation process. Use it for the improvement of your living situation so that you can create a more supportive environment for your college success. You will find this skill valuable all through life.

Journal Entry

Explore how you felt at the beginning, during, and at the end of the negotiation process.

❖ Chapter 16 ❖

Minority and International Students
Adjusting to American College Life

The purpose of this chapter is to help the minority student or the international student **(1)** define his/her unique perspective, knowledge, skills, heritage; **(2)** identify the structure and assumptions that guide successful students at his/her college or university; and **(3)** adjust his/her own attitudes and behaviors so he/she can navigate successfully in a wider range of careers and markets.

Rather than lose your minority identity, you should build on it. I am currently designing training programs to help German executives and their families transfer between Germany and the United States. When I work with Germans, I must be punctual to the second, expect planning and development to take four times longer, examine every detail again and again with exhaustive studies, and of course, learn to speak German. However, I don't give up my own identity.

In order to get on the road to success, you will have to define your minority perspective and communication style. For example, is "on time" for you exactly on time, 5 minutes late with an excuse, 30 minutes late with a casual, social entrance?

When students arrive late for my class, I remind them for their own good that I—along with their future employers in the United States—expect them to be on time. Another example of cultural differences in communication can be found in nonverbal behavior. Does listening for you imply that you are glancing up and down at the speaker (standard white American), staring at the speaker (French), avoiding eye contact (many African and third-world cultures)? Once you become aware of some of your cultural communication basics, you can gain more control over your intercultural development.

Individual Exercise 16.1 *Basic Cultural Factors*

Purpose: When you come from another culture, you bring your reality with you. As you interact in your new cultural surroundings, you may go through culture shock. Culture shock is usually a six- to nine-month process of **(1)** excitement and adventure; **(2)** depression because things just don't work right for you; **(3)** adjustment— very hard work; and **(4)** results. The degree of culture shock is not so great for the white middle-class student who moves from the country to the city as it is for the emigrée who comes to the United States for the first time with few or no English language skills. Beware of underestimating your degree of culture shock if you are moving from urban to rural, a minority in a majority system (for example, a black in a predominantly white university), or an exchange student. If you find frustration building within the first six months of college, look at the cultural differences between you and the campus society. Learn the verbal and nonverbal signals of the new system.

This exercise will help minority and international students adjust to their new cultural surroundings.

Directions: Locate two out of three: **(1)** a successful upperclassman who comes from your cultural background; **(2)** an adviser or counselor who either comes from your cultural background or who is trained to work with multicultural students; **(3)** a faculty member or administrator who is either from your cultural background or who understands the problems of multicultural students. Ask these people the following questions prefaced with your statements about your previous school experiences.

As you interview, note the other person's identification of problems and his or her suggested social strategies for solving them in the Adjustment Action Plan printed after the statements and questions. For example, if in your interview you discover that the difference between American informality and your more formal customs has made it difficult for you to "fit in" to clubs and organizations, I would recommend that you take a class in Interpersonal Communication. You would then check groups/clubs, fill in *Interpersonal Communication* under *Recommendation*, and note the date and time when you can fit the course into your academic plan. Then proceed to adjust yourself where needed. The Adjustment Action Plan is designed to help you see where you are in the process of cultural change.

Statement: At home, the relationship between students and faculty is best described as (*description and examples*):

_____

_____

Question: What is the relationship between students and faculty at this college? Formal? Informal?

_____

_____

Question: How do you arrange to see a faculty member on this campus?

_____

_____

Statement: At home, when a (class, appointment, social event) is at 10 AM one is expected to show up at _____ .

Question: What are the expected arrival times for classes, appointments, parties on this campus?

_____

_____

Statement: At home, I was interested in _____ or belonged to the following kinds of groups or organizations:

_____

_____

Question: Are there any similar groups or organizations on this campus?

_____

_____

Statement: At home, my status was_____. The three most important things in my life were/are:

_____

_____

_____

Question: How do my values and social position at home compare with social roles in this culture?

_____

_____

Question: What are the kinds of problems experienced by students like myself on this campus?

_____

_____

Question: What activities would you recommend I attend to give me a better sense of this culture?

_____

_____

Question: Who else would you suggest that I talk with about my adjustment to the culture of this campus?

_____

_____

Question: Where would I find students like myself who have succeeded on this campus?

_____

_____

Note: On your calendar or time organizer, assign yourself to see events and people that will help you with your cultural adjustment to college.

Closure: By talking with people who can appreciate that you are in transition, you can ease your adjustment considerably. If you have finished this exercise you may have already developed some relationships that will help you find your way in your new society.

Adjustment Action Plan 16.1A

Adjustment Area	Check Here	Recommendation Course/event	Time Frame for Action	Date/time Action Began	Date/time Completed
Faculty Interview					
Group Clubs					
Habits					
Values					
Expected Problems					
Other					

Individual Exercise 16.2 *Skills and Knowledge*

Purpose: In order to stay on the road to success, you must identify the skills and basic knowledge needed to travel on the road and how your skills and knowledge measure up to the standards of the market in this country. Those who have strong reading, writing, and speaking skills will be able to organize and communicate their ideas more effectively than those with weak skills. Basic skills in math, statistics, and often computers are assumed on the road to success in the United States. In-depth theoretical and factual knowledge of your specialty, with working knowledge in related areas, is necessary for success in most organizations in the United States. This exercise will help you identify the level of skill and knowledge required for success in the market and how your skills and knowledge measure up.

Directions: Before you begin, be sure to complete the study skills evaluation in Chapter 5. Meet with your adviser and the faculty member you feel most comfortable with. Complete the following statements, then ask them the questions for feedback.

Statements: In my high school the most advanced courses I took were:

_____

_____

_____

The theories and factual areas we covered included:

_____

_____

_____

An example of my best paper or report is: (Show copy if you have one; if you can, have one mailed from home, it would be worth waiting for.)

_____

_____

Question: What is expected of students at this college or university in math? In composition? In reading?

_____

_____

_____

Statement: Most of my tests in high school were: *(type)*

_____

_____

Question: What kinds of tests/assignments are typically given at this school?

_____

_____

Question: How do I compare with other students on this campus in the following areas: Math skills?

_____

English language skills?

_____

Reading comprehension?

_____

SAT scores?

_____

Any other skills that are important for my intended major?

_____

Adjustment Prescription: Consult with your adviser, study skills personnel and determine exactly what you should do to adjust your cultural and academic skills to improve your chances for success in college. Work with your adviser to fill out the action plan on the following page. Then map out your action plan on your calendar or time organizer. Some things can be accomplished in a few days, but most will require regular attention.

Adjustment Action Plan 16.2A

Adjustment Area	Check Here	Recommendation Course/event	Time Frame for Action	Date/time Action Began	Date/time Completed
Math Skills					
Reading Skills					
Writing Skills					
Language Problems					
Testing Skills					
Computer Skills					
General Background					
Study Skills					
Time Management					

Closure: If you have identified any weaknesses, feel good about it. You found it before it gave you real problems. Take your time, learn what you need to learn to succeed, and proceed. If you have identified any strengths, feel even better about it. You now know what you can build on.

Individual Exercise 16.3 *You and the Market*

Purpose: Your success in the American (and international) market depends on your ability to: **(1)** identify your unique traits and interests—do you speak a second language or know a particular social network? **(2)** identify the niche in the market where your unique traits and interests can serve a need; **(3)** identify the knowledge and skills required for success in your career area; **(4)** develop strategies for acquiring or improving the knowledge and/or skills; **(5)** develop and enact strategies for networking into the market area of your choice. This exercise will help you identify your multicultural assets and how they can be applied in the marketplace.

Directions: Complete the self-evaluation exercises in the first five chapters of this book, as well as those in Chapter 9. Pay special attention to your themes and developing your network in Chapter 9. Discuss your evaluation and networking feedback with advisers, counselors, faculty, and professionals who consider your minority or unique cultural perspective to be an asset that you can build on, rather than something you should unlearn or repress. Interview them using the following statements and questions.

Statement: I have a working knowledge of the following languages and dialects:

_____

_____

Question: Are there career areas or market needs in which my knowledge of languages or dialects or knowledge of a minority group could be an asset?

_____

_____

Statement: In my earlier years I acquired the following skills (don't leave anything out):

_____

_____

Question: How do you think these skills can be adapted to new or existing markets?

_____

_____

Statement: In my self-evaluation exercises I discovered that my themes are

_____, _____ and _____, which I have related to the following possible careers and educational goals:

_____

_____

Question: Can you think of any additional career or educational goals that might re-
             late to the themes I have defined?

_____

_____

Statement: My networking has led me to the following people who have suggested that I:

_____

_____

Question: Can you suggest anyone else I could talk to who might have good insights on
             how I could best adjust my skills, knowledge, and interests to the market-
             place?

_____

_____

Closure: Whatever knowledge you have, consider it an asset. If
you consult with an adviser who does not share your assets, don't
blame them for not recognizing your strengths. Likewise, don't de-
value your assets because others don't recognize them. Build on
your origin, don't deny it. Be sure to adjust your academic plan in
Chapter 4 according to the advice you got in your interviews.

Individual Exercise 16.4 *Minority Focus for Success*

Purpose: Minority students in the United States have some problems that are significantly different from those of international
students. Racism works as an outside force to subdue a people,
whereas confusion over cultural heritage and personal identity
prevents the individual from defining a direction based on his or
her strengths, values, and the betterment of his or her social
group. In addition, many minority students had a high school
experience that left them unprepared to enter the majority society
on a number of levels. A majority-controlled student government,
school newspaper, or yearbook may seem impenetrable to a minority student. Social organizations tend to develop along racial
lines. Although exclusive interaction with one's minority peers is
vital for the development of a heritage awareness, it can be det-

rimental to the development of personal success in the larger social and economic system. The development of a large social network—the cultivation of contacts—is a vital part of success in America. The purpose of this exercise is to help the minority student define his or her present social orientation, design strategies for expanding contacts, overcome prejudice, and apply his or her higher education in the marketplace.

Directions: The following assignments can help the minority student develop self-awareness and a wider social network. Social development takes time. This exercise may take as long as a year.

1. Interview five adults who belong to your minority. Ask them to discuss your cultural/historical heritage, the contributions that people from your minority have made to society, and their experience with racism and how to overcome it. Ask each to introduce you to a successful adult from the majority social group.
2. Interview the majority adult, asking how he or she defines success, the role of education in his or her success, and how his or her social network helped.
3. Either associate yourself with a social organization that contains a significant number of your minority or start a group, club, fraternity, or sorority. Urge your organization to cosponsor one event a term with another organization that is predominantly of the majority group.

Closure: Social groups have power that the individual alone does not possess. However, individual strength can also be found in being comfortable with, and able to move among, people from different social groups. Cultivate diversity; you will never regret it.

Individual Exercise 16.5 *Third Culture Kids or Global Nomads*

Purpose: Students who have moved from one country (culture) to another during their childhood or teen years belong to a special group with unique strengths and probably unique problems. Such students are not easily identifiable, but they are in need of special help and guidance. The purpose of this exercise is to help third culture kids (TCKs), or global nomads, identify themselves and develop the support system they need.

Directions: If you have moved from one country to another in your early or teen years, review the following list of identifying characteristics of TCKs.

Characteristics of Third Culture Kids
or Global Nomads[1]

Positives

1. World view: personal friendships in other countries—a view of the world that includes mental pictures of real people in real places resulting from relationships with people in other parts of the world.
2. Cross-cultural skills: observant, flexible, compliant, sensitive, tolerant, accepting.
3. Linguistic ability: often multilingual; even if not multilingual he or she has the advantage of having heard other languages and is confident of being able to learn other languages.
4. Maturity: often two or three years beyond peers; uncomfortable with peers; comfortable and able to communicate more readily with people several years older and with adults.

Negatives

1. Rootlessness: home is where folks are.
2. Unresolved grief/resulting sadness: usually due to separation from friends in other parts of the world.
3. Insecurity in relationships: expect breakups; experience sense of emotional distance and loneliness, usually because of short-term relationships in the past and anticipation of leaving or being left, thus maintaining an emotional distance. The TCK develops a strong sense of independence, which, if allowed to become extreme, can produce deep loneliness and an intensified sense of not belonging.
4. Culturally off balance: having the sense of not knowing signals and information that others have at their fingertips; anxiety produced by the suspicion that in a given situation one might be embarrassed or even in some kind of danger because of not

[1]Developed and presented by David C. Pollock, Executive Director, Interactions, P.O. Box 950, Fillmore, New York, 14735 - 0905 at the XIII Congress of the International Society for Intercultural Education, Training and Research, Montreal, May, 1987

knowing certain issues and information that others have as-similated in the normal process of living within a culture.

If you can identify yourself as a third culture kid who is in need of counseling and your campus does not have special help for you, contact Norma M. McCaig, Executive Director, Global Nomad Society, 30 Wellesley Circle, Glen Echo, Maryland 20812; tele-phone: (301) 229-0293. We have met and talked. I am convinced that she has a support group for you. In the meantime, contact your campus counselor—usually associated with health services. He or she may be able to help you through a rough time. And talk to your instructor and/or dean of students about starting a chapter or support group on your campus.

Closure: People with diverse cultural backgrounds have assets that most people can never dream of acquiring. Although TCKs may experience some difficulties, they also have unique back-ground and talents that outweigh their weaknesses.

Group Activity 16.6 *Racism, Culture, and Contributions*

Purpose: To help all students publicly recognize racism and ac-knowledge the value of having people from different backgrounds working together in the United States and the world.

Directions: Form a large circle and have each member of the class respond to the following questions:

1. What is one example of racism in this country, and how is it reflected in the organization of this campus?
2. Give an example of a contribution made by a member of a mi-nority which has benefited many people.
3. What can we do on this campus to promote an appreciation of all people?

Closure: This activity should help you focus on the problems of racism on campus and bring your class together in open discussion on how and why things should be changed.

Journal Entry

Discuss how you feel about the relationship between social groups on campus and in the larger society. Are you prejudiced against others?

❖ Chapter 17 ❖
_____

Drugs and Alcohol
Your Choice

In *College Is Only the Beginning* (1989), Michael Shaver and Reid Montgomery, Jr. discuss the decisions facing freshmen today when they encounter drugs and alcohol on campus. The exercises and activities in this chapter are designed to give you honest information on behaviors related to drug and alcohol use and abuse. In addition, some of the activities are also useful for developing an awareness of responsible drinking. Learning how to drink or deciding not to drink should be considered a critical part of your education, because this aspect of your behavior will have a direct bearing on your life in society.

Individual Exercise 17.1 *What Are the Signs of Alcoholism?*

Purpose: The purpose of this exercise is to help you establish some clear measurement of where you stand on one of the biggest problems facing our young people today: addiction.

Directions: The following questions will help you learn whether you have some of the symptoms of alcoholism or drug addiction.

You may use the questionnaire as a rough checklist to determine whether you, your friend, or a family member need help. Check yes or no in response to the following questions.[1] If you use drugs other than alcohol, substitute the words *drinking* with *using*, *drunk* with *high*, and *alcoholism* with *addiction*.

Yes　No

_____ _____　1.　Do you occasionally drink heavily after a disappointment, quarrel, or when the boss gives you a hard time?

_____ _____　2.　When you have trouble or feel under pressure, do you always drink more heavily than usual?

_____ _____　3.　Have you noticed that you are able to handle more liquor than you did when you were first drinking?

_____ _____　4.　Did you ever wake up on the "morning after" and discover that you could not remember part of the evening before, even though your friends tell you that you did not pass out?

_____ _____　5.　When drinking with others, do you try to have a few extra drinks when others will not know it?

_____ _____　6.　Are there certain occasions when you feel uncomfortable if alcohol is not available?

_____ _____　7.　Have you recently noticed that when you begin drinking you are in more of a hurry to get a first drink than you used to be?

_____ _____　8.　Are you secretly irritated when your family or friends discuss your drinking?

_____ _____　9.　Have you recently noticed an increase in the frequency of your memory blackouts?

_____ _____　10.　Do you often find that you wish to continue drinking after your friends say they have had enough?

_____ _____　11.　Do you usually have a reason for the occasions when you drink heavily?

_____ _____　12.　When you are sober, do you often regret things you have done or said while drinking?

_____ _____　13.　Have you tried switching brands or following different plans for controlling your drinking?

_____ _____　14.　Have you often failed to keep the promises you have made to yourself about controlling or cutting down on your drinking?

_____ _____　15.　Have you ever tried to control your drinking by making a change in schools or getting new friends?

_____ _____　16.　Do you try to avoid family or close friends while you are drinking?

_____ _____　17.　Are you having an increasing number of financial and school problems?

_____ _____　18.　Do more people seem to be treating you unfairly without good reason?

_____ _____　19.　Do you eat very little or irregularly when you are drinking?

[1]"What Kind of Drinker Are You?" Reprinted by permission of the National Council on Alcoholism, Inc., New York.

Yes   No

		20.	Do you sometimes have the "shakes" in the morning and find that it helps to have a little drink?

_____ _____ **20.** Do you sometimes have the "shakes" in the morning and find that it helps to have a little drink?

_____ _____ **21.** Have you recently noticed that you cannot drink as much as you once did?

_____ _____ **22.** Do you sometimes stay drunk for several days at a time?

_____ _____ **23.** Do you sometimes feel very depressed and wonder whether life is worth living?

_____ _____ **24.** Sometimes after periods of drinking, do you see or hear things that aren't there?

_____ _____ **25.** Do you get terribly frightened after you have been drinking heavily?

If you answered yes to any of the questions, you have some of the symptoms that may indicate alcoholism. Yes answers to several of the questions indicate the following stages of alcoholism:

Questions 1–8: Early stage

Questions 9–21: Middle stage

Questions 22–25: The beginning of the final stage of alcoholism

Closure: Everybody has problems at one time or another. If this exercise indicates that you have a drinking or drug problem, get help now. Contact the director of your college's student health services. Problems don't go away by themselves.

Individual Exercise 17.2 *Value Continuum*

Purpose: The use of alcohol and drugs has increased among young people to the extent that one in four has a drinking problem. Drug use among young people is still increasing. You should define where you stand before you get into it so that you can decide for yourself before you are tempted. If you are already using drugs and/or alcohol, answer honestly and see how your positions differ from your peers'.

Directions: Place an X along the continuum to indicate your position.[2]

---

[2]Adapted from materials provided by James Cox, Dickinson College.

Value Continuum 17.2A

Left	1	2	3	4	5	Right
There should be complete freedom to drink.	1	2	3	4	5	There should be complete restrictions on drinking.
There should be complete freedom to use drugs.	1	2	3	4	5	There should be complete restrictions on using drugs.
It is perfectly OK to drink and drive.	1	2	3	4	5	One should never drink and drive.
It is perfectly OK to use drugs and drive.	1	2	3	4	5	One should never use drugs and drive.
It is enjoyable to be around people who are drinking.	1	2	3	4	5	People who are drinking should be avoided.
It is enjoyable to be around people who are using drugs.	1	2	3	4	5	People who are using drugs should be avoided.
You should not be held responsible for your actions if you have been drinking.	1	2	3	4	5	You are responsible for all your actions even when drinking.
You should not be held responsible for your actions if you have been using drugs.	1	2	3	4	5	You are responsible for all your actions even when using drugs.
The host of a party should not interfere with a guest's drinking behavior.	1	2	3	4	5	The host of a party is responsible for limiting a guest's alcohol consumption.
The host of a party should not interfere with a guest's drug use.	1	2	3	4	5	The host of a party is responsible for limiting guest's drug use.
I have no responsibility to tell a friend that he/she has a drinking or a drug problem.	1	2	3	4	5	I am compelled to point out a drug or drinking problem to a friend.
I could never become a problem drinker, alcoholic, or drug addict.	1	2	3	4	5	I am, or will become, a problem drinker, alcoholic, or drug addict.

Closure: This exercise is the first step in getting honest feedback that can help you clarify exactly where you stand on the issue. Continue with Activity 17.3 to establish a sense of acceptable and unacceptable actions in regard to the use of drugs and alcohol among your peers.

Group Activity 17.3 *Value Discussion*

Purpose: The purpose of this activity is to help each student get a sense of others' values that affect their thinking about using drugs and alcohol.

Directions: Form groups of no more than five. Compare your responses to Exercise 17.2. When there is a difference of more than one point between the value indicators of the group members, the members of the group should share their reasons for their judgment. After the groups have completed their discussions, each group should have one member write on the board the group's majority and minority positions. Then the class at large should give reasons in support of the positions on the board. **Rule:** During the entire activity, only "I" statements are permitted. That is, each individual is allowed to make statements only about his or her own judgments or examples. Class members should avoid negative value judgments about other students' positions. Questions that clarify the position of another student are permissible.

Closure: A sense of social responsibility is a good sign of maturity. The kind of exchange that you had in this activity helps you develop this social sense and may improve the health and safety of all in our society.

Group Activity 17.4 *Developing Consensus About Drinking*

Purpose: The purpose of this activity is to give you practice in making value judgments about drugs and alcohol in social situations.

Directions: In the United States we do not have a consensus as to what constitutes responsible drinking behavior. Thus controversy and confusion surround the definition of problem drinking and sanctions against irresponsible drinking.

Please rank the following examples from 1 (least responsible drinking behavior) to 5 (most responsible drinking behavior).[3] Then, within the class, discuss your ranking and attempt to arrive at a consensus ranking.

A_____
Linda has just left the party and is taking a friend home. Her blood alcohol concentration of .10 is the legal definition of intoxication in most states. She is weaving erratically down the street and almost crashes into an oncoming car.

B_____
Sam really likes mixed drinks and about twice a week in his room will make himself several drinks, using his favorite 80 proof liquor (40 percent alcohol). Sometimes he has more than several and completely misses dinner.

C_____
Frank, having been frustrated all day, goes to the local bar that evening and drinks six beers in one hour. Frank weighs about 150 pounds. His blood alcohol concentration is about .09. He gets angry and starts a fight by breaking a bottle over the head of a much larger man sitting next to him.

D_____
Already feeling high, a group of friends on their way to a party decide to chug that most consumed alcoholic libation in America, beer. Before leaving, one of the friends pulls an overhead light from its fixture. Laughing, the others start to wrestle and, in falling against a trophy case cabinet, they break the glass.

E_____
Sandy, a graduate student who is divorced and living with her small child, is becoming an alcoholic (one of the 15 percent of all Americans who drink very irresponsibly). She drinks beer throughout most of the day. One afternoon a friend stops by to visit and finds her asleep amid an unkempt living room and the child crying and hungry in her crib.

Closure: Value judgments are difficult at first, but you must make them. Be honest with your personal values.

---

[3]Source: Lambda Chi Alpha fraternity Alcohol Awareness Kit, supplied by James Cox, Dickinson College. Used by permission.

Group Activity 17.5 *Getting Answers About Drugs*

Purpose: As freshmen you are entering a new society with its own values and problems. National studies tell us that 25 percent of young Americans are using drugs or alcohol from the fourth grade on through high school. Cocaine, nicotine, marijuana, LSD, speed, sopors, crack, uppers, downers, mescaline, mushrooms, hashish, and heroin have different levels of popularity and supply in different regions of our country. You may or may not have experimented or seen others experiment with any of these and other drugs. Regardless of your experience, you may not understand what these drugs do to your body and your mind.

The level of drug use is directly proportional to the level of one's education about drugs—because educated people understand what drugs do to their health. The purpose of this activity is to begin to raise your educational level in regard to what drugs do to your body and your mind. I have seen close friends "enjoy" drugs until the drugs had taken over their lives, destroyed their marriages, their careers, broken their health, and in some cases, left them in prison. Learn now and avoid the pain later.

Directions: Assume that no one in your class uses drugs but that everyone has heard of or seen some drugs being used. Have your class list on the chalkboard the drugs that you think you should know about. Assign at least one student to investigate the effects of each drug on the body and the mind. Investigate by interviewing and soliciting pamphlets from your student health center, drug rehabilitation centers, local hospitals, professors of chemistry, biology, pharmacy, or nursing, and government agencies on the local and national levels. Fill out the information form in this activity. Compare your information with other students' findings.

Discussion: Once you have shared your information about drugs, everyone in the class should attempt to answer the questions: Why do people use (a particular drug). Try to determine whether the individual is under pressure and trying to escape; is addicted and can't quit; is under peer pressure to use the drug; or just uses it without the knowledge of what he/she is doing to him/herself. What effect does (the drug in question) have on the human body?

If you want to have an impact on the drug problem, hold a poster contest in which students graphically illustrate the effects a particular drug has on the body and mind. Display the best posters in your student union and distribute the others around your campus.

Drug Information Form 17.5A

Name of drug: _____

Sources used for information:

_____

_____

_____

Chart of chemicals in the drug and their effects on the body and mind. (Continue on another page if necessary.)

Chemicals	Effects on your body	Effects on your mind
_____	_____	_____
_____	_____	_____
_____	_____	_____
_____	_____	_____
_____	_____	_____
_____	_____	_____
_____	_____	_____

Closure: The slide down is always easier than the climb up. But the view is always better at the top. Understand the direction that you are really going. If your goals are to acquire a good education and become successful and you are using a drug, you are acting against your goals. If you need help, see your campus health officer or counselor or call the hotlines (such as Narcotics Anonymous) that are listed in your local phone book and Yellow Pages.

Journal Entry

Respond to the following: How do your feelings about your use of drugs/alcohol compare to the feelings of other members of your class?

❖ Chapter 18 ❖

Benchmarks for Health and Fitness

We all need a proper diet and exercise; without the combination of the two, your body cannot do its best for you. In *College Is Only the Beginning*, Linda Morphis presents good advice on how to improve your nutritional intake and your exercise quotient. Rather than repeat her contribution, I am presenting the following exercises and activities as a way of establishing benchmarks in nutrition and health. Here you will find ways to establish your most healthful weight, an analysis of your eating habits, ways of getting exercise through everyday activities, and a record of your fitness improvement as you exercise.

Individual Exercise 18.1 *Your Optimum Weight*

Purpose: The following chart is to be used as a means of determining the weight for lowest mortality for your frame size.[1] The purpose of determining your optimum weight is to give you a benchmark on your state of nutritional health. Your optimum weight is not the only indicator of nutritional health, but it is a good one.

---

[1]Reprinted with permission of Ross Laboratories, Columbus, Ohio, from *Dietetic Currents* 10, no. 4, ©1983 Ross Laboratories.

Directions: Follow the instructions below to determine your optimum weight for your frame size. Once you determine the weight at which you (statistically) will live the longest, continue on to the subsequent exercises to see whether your eating habits conform with good nutritional practices.

Determination of Body-Frame Size

The revised height and weight tables list weight ranges for men and women aged 25 to 59 years, while allowing for differences in body frames. Body frame is designated as small, medium, or large and is based on elbow breadth. This method of approximating frame size is given below:

1. Extend one arm and bend the forearm upward at a 90-degree angle. Keep the fingers straight and turn the inside of the wrist toward the body.
2. Place the thumb and index finger of the other hand on the two prominent bones on either side of the elbow.
3. Measure the space between the fingers against a ruler or a tape measure. For a more accurate measurement, use a caliper.
4. Compare the measurement with those measurements listed in the table. This gives the elbow measurements for medium-framed men and women of various heights. Measurements lower than those listed in the table indicate a small frame, whereas measurements higher indicate a large frame.

Men		Women	
Height (1" heels)	Elbow Breadth	Height (1" heels)	Elbow Breadth
5'2"–5'3"	2-1/2"–2-7/8"	4'10"–4'11"	2-1/4"–2-1/2"
5'4"–5'7"	2-5/8"–2-7/8"	5'0"–5'3"	2-1/4"–2-1/2"
5'8"–5'11"	2-3/4"–3"	5'4"–5'7"	2-3/8"–2-5/8"
6'0"–6'3"	2-3/4"–3-1/8"	5'8"–5'11"	2-3/8"–2-5/8"
6'4"	2-7/8"–3-1/4"	6'0"	2-1/2–2-3/4"

Source: Metropolitan Life Insurance Company

1983 Height and Weight Tables: Men

| Height | | | Frame[1] | |
Feet	Inches	Small	Medium	Large
5	2	128–134	131–141	138–150
5	3	130–136	133–143	140–153
5	4	132–138	135–145	142–156
5	5	134–140	137–148	144–160
5	6	136–142	139–151	146–164
5	7	138–145	142–154	149–168
5	8	140–148	145–157	152–172
5	9	142–151	148–160	155–176
5	10	144–154	151–163	158–180
5	11	146–157	154–166	161–184
6	0	149–160	157–170	164–188
6	1	152–164	160–174	168–192
6	2	155–168	164–178	172–197
6	3	158–172	167–182	176–202
6	4	162–176	171–187	181–207

1983 Height and Weight Tables: Women

| Height | | | Frame[1] | |
Feet	Inches	Small	Medium	Large
4	10	102–111	109–121	118–131
4	11	103–113	111–123	120–134
5	0	104–115	113–126	122–137
5	1	106–118	115–129	125–140
5	2	108–121	118–132	128–143
5	3	111–124	121–135	131–147
5	4	114–127	124–138	134–151
5	5	117–130	127–141	137–155
5	6	120–133	130–144	140–159
5	7	123–136	133–147	143–163
5	8	126–139	136–150	146–167
5	9	129–142	139–153	149–170
5	10	132–145	142–156	152–173
5	11	135–148	145–159	155–176
6	0	138–151	148–162	158–179

[1]Weights at ages 25–59 based on lowest mortality, according to frame, in indoor clothing weighing five pounds, shoes with one-inch heels.

Closure: Optimum weight is not necessarily the most fashionable or most effective for job performance. It is simply the weight at which the insurance industry has determined statistically that you will live the longest. If longevity is one of your life goals, you should consider it.

Individual Exercise 18.2 *The Food Diary*

Purpose: This exercise is designed to help you become more conscious of what you eat and why you eat it. We eat because we are hungry, nervous, celebrating, with a friend, lonely. The first stage in getting control over your nutrition and weight is developing an understanding of your eating patterns and motivations.

Directions: Fill in the categories of Food Intake Inventory Form 18.2A for one week. The form should supply you with enough space for a record of one day's meals. You might want to photocopy the form before you write in it so that you can use it for the entire week. Identify the patterns that emerge after one week.

Answer the following questions by referring to the information you have gathered on your eating habits.

1. What three foods do you eat the most and what are the two main ingredients in these foods?

    Foods   **Ingredients**

    1. _____   A. _____   B._____

    2. _____   A. _____   B._____

    3. _____   A. _____   B._____

2. How many times do you eat a day? _____

3. How do you feel before and when you are eating; that is, what is your usual motivation

    for eating? _____

4. Do you eat a balanced diet? _____

5. What are the four food groups and what should you eat from each on a daily basis?

    _____

    _____

_____

_____

6. State one thing you can do to improve your eating habits. _____

_____

_____

Closure: This exercise should have helped you become more aware of the food that you eat. We are often surprised at the ingredients in some of our foods. Be responsible for what you eat. After all, you are what you eat.

Group Activity 18.3 *Creating Exercise in Your Day*

Purpose: Studies show that young Americans are more out of shape than ever. In China the elevators are for foreign visitors, the stairs for the Chinese. There, from a philosophy that combines economy, conservation, and personal fitness, a lifestyle that leads one to the stairs has been born. If we look at our daily actions we can find that we often cause ourselves expense by avoiding exercise. Most people who have to move themselves from one place to another to accomplish their daily tasks can significantly increase their fitness by changing their travel habits, load-carrying habits, and, of course, eating habits.

The purpose of this activity is to help you adjust some of your more modern habits to allow for a little old-fashioned exercise in your daily routine.

Food Intake Inventory Form 18.2A

Food	How much	Time	Where are you? Home (room) Work Restaurant Recreation Activity engaged in	Who is with you?	How do you feel? A-Anxious F-____ B-Bored G-____ C-Tired D-Depressed E-Angry

Adapted from *Behavioral Control—A New Self-Help Approach to Weight Control*, Extension Bulletin E 781, Cooperative Extension Service, Michigan State University.

Directions: The members of the class should assign three to five students to the central evaluating committee (CEC). Each class participant devises a way to change a normal activity to an activity that includes a modest amount of exercise the average person can do. For example, one might consider using the stairs instead of the elevator. Use the Activity Proposal Form 18.3A to prepare your suggested activity for presentation.

As each student presents an activity, the CEC should assign a degree of difficulty (DOD) number between 1 and 5. For example, taking the elevator one flight might be assigned a degree of difficulty 1, whereas walking two miles to school with a pack of books on your back could earn a 5.

At the next class meeting, after the CEC performs their evaluating task, they must produce a compendium of all redesigned activities with their DOD assigned. The compendium should contain all of the activity descriptions with an identifying number assigned to each. They should distribute a copy of the compendium to each class participant. Their task will be reduced to a simple cut/paste and photocopy or ditto process if each participant hands in a neatly typed or printed description on the form. To increase the activity options for your class, you may want to combine your efforts with one or more seminars and develop one large compendium of activities.

Note: Although this activity can be performed purely for enjoyment, those with a competitive spirit can easily turn it into a contest by comparing totals from the Physical Activity Record 18.3B To create a competitive situation that may inspire more to participate in exercise, distribute the compendium of activities with DOD assigned to each activity. Establish a time period for a contest. I suggest at least one month, because some students might require a week or two to get into an exercise mode. As you record your activity during the contest period, be sure to multiply your DOD times 2. This device is used to inspire the contestants to aspire to the harder activities, because doubling a 5 gives you a much greater score than doubling a 2. At the conclusion of the contest period, participating groups should add up their scores and acknowledge the highest and most improved scores.

After any sustained vigorous exercise, be sure to record the activity and your heart rate on Physical Activity Record 18.3B. You will notice that, as you continue to exercise over weeks and months, your heart rate will decrease because exercise improves the efficiency of your cardiovascular system.

Activity Proposal Form 18.3A

	Old Activity	Replacement Activity	Suggested DOD
Title:			☐ Approved
Description:			☐ Changed
Distance traveled:			☐ DOD changed to:
Travel method:			
Weight carried:			
Additional information:			

Closure: While this activity is designed for inspiring some modest exercise in an otherwise sedentary day, I also encourage you to engage in some vigorous activity several times a week. As Linda Morphis suggests, you can check your heartbeat to discover your fitness or rate of improvement. See her chapter in *College Is Only the Beginning* for exact instructions on how to measure your fitness by your heartbeat. Your results can also be recorded on the Physical Activity Record. It's always encouraging to see your results!

Journal Entry

Write several paragraphs describing your present state of fitness and how you feel about it. Do you want to improve it? If so, how?

Physical Activity Record 18.3B

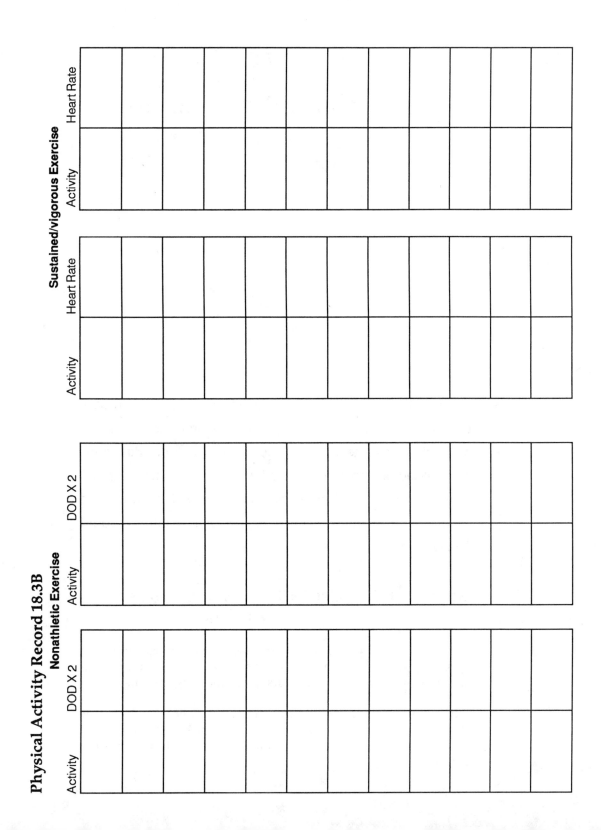

❖ Chapter 19 ❖

Identifying Your Stress

This chapter is designed to help you identify, monitor, and control your stress. Freshmen are especially prone to stress because they are entering a new society that is filled with strangers, based on competition, laced with time management problems, twice as demanding as high school, and charged with the emotional pain that often accompanies new interpersonal relationships.

Individual Exercise 19.1 *Freshman Stress Factors*

Purpose: Although many factors and situations contribute to freshman stress, the five listed on the following page are regarded by many college health officers as the most significant.

Directions: Review the stress factors that follow and arrange them in order of their impact on you. Assign 1 to the factor that has the greatest impact on you, 5 to the factor with the least impact on you.

Freshman Stress Factors[1]

_____ **Separation from family**
Separation can be a positive or negative experience for a student. Your family is not around to share your triumphs and failures; nobody is there to remind you what to do and when to do it. You have to find new support systems to replace those left behind. That's not easy.

_____ **Freedom**
For most campuses, long gone are strict dorm rules, dress codes, and mandatory class attendance. Now you have to make your own decisions, look closely at your life, and readjust your own values.

_____ **Competition**
Increased pressure results from grade competition, graduate school slots, and jobs. Competition adds to the feeling of loneliness because so much time is spent working in isolation.

_____ **Peer pressure**
You seek acceptance in a new environment. It may mean conforming to a friend's attitudes toward alcohol, drugs, partying, or study. Sexual pressures may also develop.

_____ **Choosing a career**
What approach do you take? Do you major in a subject that interests you or enter the field that your parents have pegged for you? What about the job market, and will the job pay off later? Will financial pressures force you to make quick, premature decisions?

Closure: Ask your adviser and counselor for ideas on how you can best adjust to the greatest stress factor in your freshman experience.

Individual Exercise 19.2 _General Vulnerability to Stress_

Purpose: There are a number of ways to arrange your life to reduce or increase your vulnerability to stress. A testing situation is not stressful in itself. The way you approach the test will determine how much stress you will experience. This exercise is designed to

---

[1]James Cox, Dickinson College, and Barbara Galderise, Duquesne University, "Stress Management." Used by permission.

increase your awareness of the factors that contribute to your stress, as well as what proportion the factors play in your experience. After you increase your awareness (know yourself a little better), you can begin to control your stress level.

Directions: Score each item from 1 (almost always) to 5 (never), according to how much of the time each statement applies to you.[2]

____ **1.** I eat at least one hot, balanced meal a day.

____ **2.** I get seven to eight hours of sleep at least four nights a week.

____ **3.** I give and receive affection regularly.

____ **4.** I have at least one relative within 50 miles on whom I can rely.

____ **5.** I exercise to the point of perspiration at least twice a week.

____ **6.** I smoke less than half a pack of cigarettes a day.

____ **7.** I have fewer than five alcoholic drinks a week.

____ **8.** I am the appropriate weight for my height.

____ **9.** I have an income adequate to meet basic expenses.

____**10.** I get strength from my religious beliefs.

____**11.** I regularly attend clubs or social activities.

____**12.** I have a network of friends and acquaintances.

____**13.** I have one or more friends to confide in about personal matters.

____**14.** I am in good health (including eyesight, hearing, teeth).

____**15.** I am able to speak openly about my feelings when angry or worried.

____**16.** I have regular conversations with the people I live with about domestic problems, such as chores, money, and daily living issues.

____**17.** I do something for fun at least once a week.

____**18.** I am able to organize my time effectively.

____**19.** I drink fewer than three cups of coffee (or tea or cola drinks) a day.

____**20.** I take quiet time for myself during the day.

Note: To get your score, add up the figures and subtract 20. Any number over 30 indicates a vulnerability to stress. You are seri-

---

[2] "Vulnerability Scale" from the *Stress Audit*, developed by Lyle H. Miller and Alma Dell Smith. Copyright 1983, Biobehavioral Associates, Brookline, Mass., reprinted with permission.

ously vulnerable if your score is between 50 and 75, and extremely vulnerable if it is over 75.

Closure: If your score is over 50, you should discuss it with your adviser or counselor. The best way to improve your score is to select two or three items at a time and try to reduce your rating by 2.

Individual Exercise 19.3 *Student Stress Factors*

Purpose: In Exercises 19.1 and 19.2 you should have identified some possible events that could be associated with stress in your life. This exercise is designed to help you identify the typical college student stress events and evaluate them to determine the level of impact they may be associated with in your college experience.

Directions: On the following page is a list of events that occur in the life of a college student.[3] Place a check in the left-hand column for each event that has happened to you during the last 12 months.

Closure: If your stress level is reaching the top of borderline or higher, you should visit your counseling center and discuss your score with a person who is trained in ways of developing strategies for coping with stress—a counselor.

Group Activity 19.4 *Strategies for Reducing Stress*

Purpose: Some excellent stress reduction exercises are available, like those offered by Kevin King in *College Is Only the Beginning*. Some ways we reduce our stress are unique to our culture. Americans have taken up jogging, aerobics, and other fitness regimens in record numbers in the past decade. Such activities help you let out your nervous energy, think thoughts at random and often socialize with others. Other ways of reducing stress are direct outgrowths of our environment. An urban campus may have more cultural and recreational facilities adjacent to it, while a campus in the Rocky Mountains offers very different stress reduction activities. One purpose of this activity is to help you identify and partake of many of the opportunities your campus offers.

[1]Barbara Galderise, "Freshman Stress Factors," Dickinson College. Used by permission.

Life Event	Point Values
_____ Death of a close family member	100
_____ Jail term	80
_____ Final year or first year in college	63
_____ Pregnancy (to you or caused by you)	60
_____ Severe personal illness or injury	53
_____ Marriage	50
_____ Any interpersonal problems	45
_____ Financial difficulties	40
_____ Death of a close friend	40
_____ Arguments with your roommate (more than every other day)	40
_____ Major disagreements with your family	40
_____ Major change in personal habits	30
_____ Change in living environment	30
_____ Beginning or ending a job	30
_____ Problems with your boss or professor	25
_____ Outstanding personal achievement	25
_____ Failure in some course	25
_____ Final exams	20
_____ Increased or decreased dating	20
_____ Change in your major	20
_____ Change in your sleeping habits	18
_____ Several-day vacation	15
_____ Change in eating habits	15
_____ Family reunion	15
_____ Change in recreational activities	15
_____ Minor illness or injury	15
_____ Minor violations of the law	11

Score: _____

Stress level: 300 + = too high—reduce stress now
150–300 = borderline—watch it
000–150 = low level—maintain

The second purpose is to help each freshman class adjust the campus environment to their particular coping needs. If your college's institutions address your needs, you will have less to worry about. For example, AIDS, drugs, new career developments, reduced reading power from TV watching, and intercultural conflicts from population shifts may be just some of the new problems facing your class. If previous classes have not had these problems, your college faculty and administrators will first have to identify the existence of such problems and then design solutions to cope with them. In some cases the identification and design phases take several years—by which time you could be a casualty of the problem. In this activity you can help your college serve your needs by identifying and suggesting solutions that might work for you.

Directions: Review the following list by yourself and circle those resources or activities that could help you reduce your stress.[4] Review the list with an upperclassman and perhaps your adviser to determine whether the resources that you identified are in place. Consult with the upperclassman and develop additional suggestions for the list that you might want to propose in class. See Group Activity 19.5 for a continuation of this exercise.

Resources	Activities
counseling center	postpone fraternity rush to second semester
intercollegiate sports	schedule short fall break before Thanksgiving
intramural program	better upperclassman housing
fraternities/sororities	additional social options
tutors	reading periods between classes and finals
career counseling	more information about campus activities
orientation program	drop finals in some courses
freshman advisers	better selection process for freshman roommate
resident assistants	improved faculty-student relations
friends	professional counselor for residents or commuters
off-campus living options	more clubs
new gym	more weekend retreats
rush counselors	lectures on how to study, coping with stress
freshman "playfair"	alcohol and drug awareness programs
alumni contacts	career-oriented aspects of individual courses
hot line—emotions	vigorous activity and frequent trips—foot, cycle, car
off-campus studies	lecture series: high school to college adjustment
music, art, creativity	student self-help groups

[4]James A. Boytim and C. Timothy Dickel, "The Counselor as Advocate of Primary Prevention: A Workshop," handout, 1987. Used by permission.

Resources	Activities
study abroad	staggered course requirement deadlines
religious services	more professor-student conferences
admission tours	organizations for "independents"
brother-sister floors	snack bar freebies at midnight (exam week)
religious services	take a "healthy personality" course
big-buddy system	late-night library study hours
writing center	study guides from professors for finals
small classes	campus security escort services
internships	senior seminars
AA or NA chapter	weight control support group
pass/fail option	human sexuality workshops
"W" options	how to study workshops
meal plan options	desegregate cafeteria tables
special-interest housing	family planning services on campus
single-room options	more nonfraternity male-female interactions
freshman seminars	better resident-commuter interaction
independent study	drug counseling
independent research	strict enforcement of quiet hours
honors program	anti-prejudice and openness seminars
dorm contracts	informal courses to improve men-women relations
test anxiety sessions	student-faculty committees

Closure: Once you have identified a way to improve campus life continue on to the next activity. If you are having coping problems, the lists in this exercise could become a good resource for your needs.

Group Activity 19.5 *Submitting Your Suggestions*

Purpose: This activity is designed to (1) organize student awareness of stress-related problems—which can include any problem facing a freshman; (2) help students discover existing and new solutions for the problems; (3) help students communicate their awareness of the problems and suggest solutions to the action center of their college or university.

Directions: Assign one student to be the brainstorming leader. Divide the rest of the class into groups of three or four with the instructor in one of the small groups. Each group member may submit one stress related problem to the group that he or she believes to be both significant and unsolved on campus. The members of the group must agree on two or more problems that meet those criteria.

After the problems are selected, each group must follow these brainstorming rules:

1. One group member should act as recorder, in addition to brainstorming.
2. The leader should focus the group on one problem at a time.
3. Free-associate and come up with as many solutions as possible.
4. The more ridiculous, original, or illogical solutions should be *encouraged*.
5. When ideas slow down, the leader should move the group to another problem.
6. Focusing on problem 2 may give you an idea for problem 1. Fine—do it.
7. Allow 15 minutes for the complete brainstorming session.

Bringing It Together

1. After 15 minutes of brainstorming, have each recorder report to the class.
2. The class leader should record the small-group results on the board.
3. If new ideas are generated—fine.
4. Any student may attach an idea to a brainstorm list by writing it out with the original problem printed at the top of the page.
5. The class leader should proceed until feedback is recorded from everyone and any additional comments are handed in.
6. The class leader should then have each group nominate one solution for high visibility that meets the following criteria:
   a. The solution is needed because the problem is significant.
   b. The solution would be attractive to the students who need it.
   c. The solution would be cost effective and fairly easy to implement.
7. Those solutions nominated by each group should be placed in an envelope marked "class priorities."
8. All solutions should be turned over to the class instructor for distribution to the proper areas of your institution.

Closure: You are a part of your college. It can serve your needs only if you present them properly within the system. This activity will help you work in large systems now and later in life.

Journal Entry

Discuss the most stressful thing in your life and the strategies you plan to use to cope with the situation.

❖ Chapter 20 ❖

Assertiveness

A Word in Time Saves Nine

In our competitive society, some people—in the pursuit of selfish goals—take on aggressive behavior, which often infringes on the rights and space of others. Assertive people protect their rights when they are confronted by aggressive individuals. Assertive behavior is as easy to take on as any behavior that you exhibit right now. Like anything else, it takes a little practice before you can feel comfortable with it. This chapter is designed to give you the practice and feedback you need to begin to develop a more assertive approach to your communication style. After a little while, you will find that you are more comfortable with the style and more satisfied with the results.

In *College Is Only the Beginning*, Ruthann Fox-Hines discusses the vital role of communication skills in assertive behavior—especially in choosing the proper response in a confrontation. The exercises and activities that follow will help you use the assertive response at the right time.

Individual Exercise 20.1 *How Assertive Are You?*

Purpose: Assertive behavior is easy for some of us in some situations and difficult in other instances. A professor may easily assert himself or herself when talking with a student but have difficulty when bargaining for agreement with a colleague. Likewise, students may be comfortable when asserting themselves with old friends but cautious and somewhat timid when working things out with a new roommate or classmate. The questionnaire that follows covers a number of typical situations in which most people find themselves reluctant to be assertive. As you review the questions, try to think of specific examples in your experience that illustrate your behavior style.

Directions: Write yes or no in the space before each question. In the next activity, the class will review the answers that an assertive person should be able to give, which can be found at the end of this chapter.

Assertiveness Questionnaire[1]

_____   1. When a person is blatantly unfair, do you usually fail to say something about it to him or her?

_____   2. Are you always very careful to avoid all trouble with other people?

_____   3. Do you often avoid social contacts for fear of doing or saying the wrong thing?

_____   4. If a friend betrays your confidence, do you tell him or her how you really feel?

_____   5. Would you insist that a roommate do his or her fair share of cleaning?

_____   6. When a clerk in a store waits on someone who has come in after you, do you call his or her attention to the matter?

_____   7. Do you find that there are very few people with whom you can be relaxed and have a good time?

_____   8. Would you be hesitant about asking a good friend to lend you a few dollars?

_____   9. If someone who has borrowed $5 from you seems to have forgotten about it, would you remind this person?

_____ 10. If a person keeps on teasing you, do you have difficulty expressing your annoyance or displeasure?

_____ 11. Would you remain standing at the rear of the crowded auditorium rather than look for a seat up front?

_____ 12. If someone kept kicking the back of your chair in a movie, would you ask him or her to stop?

_____ 13. If a friend keeps calling you very late each evening, would you ask him or her not to call after a certain time?

---

[1]Arnold A. Lazarus, "Assertive Questionnaire," in *Behavior Theory and Beyond* (New York: McGraw-Hill, 1971). Reprinted by permission of the publisher.

_____ 14. If someone starts talking to someone else right in the middle of your conversation, do you express your irritation?

_____ 15. In a plush restaurant, if you order a medium steak and find it too rare, would you ask the waiter to have it recooked?

_____ 16. If a landlord of your apartment fails to make certain necessary repairs after promising to do so, would you insist on it?

_____ 17. Would you return a faulty garment you purchased a few days ago?

_____ 18. If someone you respect expresses opinions you strongly disagree with, would you venture to state your own point of view?

_____ 19. Are you usually able to say no when people make unreasonable requests?

_____ 20. Do you think that people should stand up for their rights?

Group Activity 20.2 *Reviewing the Questionnaire*

Purpose: We all can recall situations in our past in which we wish we had acted differently. We live and learn. One way to begin to improve your assertive behavior is to review your past nonassertive episodes and realize how complications can develop when you allow your rights to go unobserved by others. The purpose of this activity is to give the class participants a chance to share some of their past and begin to imagine how they might have acted if they had been thinking more assertively.

Directions: The questionnaire may have reminded you of some instances in your own life. With the class, including the instructor, sitting in a circle, recall a situation that you or a friend ended up in because you did not employ assertive behavior. If you do not elect to participate, you have every right to "pass" when your turn comes.

After the past instances are shared, suggestions should be offered by the group as to how assertive behavior could be introduced to avoid such situations in the future.

Closure: At the end of this activity you will realize that few people are good at using assertive behavior. Together you can learn, support each other in practice, and respect each other more in your future communication.

Group Activity 20.3 *Assertive Behavior Role-Plays*

Purpose: As I stated before, the best way to learn new behavior is to practice it. Most freshmen run into the same kinds of situations with new relationships, with roommates and classmates, so this activity is designed to prepare freshmen to be more assertive in typical situations that will have long-lasting repercussions for them in their new social sphere. In addition, the more the members of the freshman class become aware of the concept and use of assertive behavior, the more they will tend to respect each other's rights, and expect and respect the assertive behavior of others.

Directions: Form groups of three. The three students should take turns trying out the roles in the following role-plays. Two should act out the roles, while the third observes and makes note of behaviors (verbal and nonverbal) that are positive assertive actions. Work on three role plays until you feel comfortable with them, then try them out for the rest of the class. The class can play the observer role and give feedback at the end of each role-play. *Note:* As you take on each role, ask yourself, "What are my rights and how should I assert them?"

Role Plays

1. The Notebook

Student A: You were a good student in high school and want to get good grades in your first term of college. You lent your classmate a notebook, because he/she missed the last class, with the understanding that he/she would bring it back to the next class—the day before the first quiz. You know that "B" is a commuter and has a hard time with this class—so you wish to help him/her if you can. When the class meets again, B is not there but a neighboring student tells you that B was not feeling well and will try to bring your notebook in next week. You don't know what is the matter with B but you do feel that he/she could have sent the notebook in with the neighbor. You have B's phone number and you are going to call and state that you are coming over for your notebook.

Student B: You were not a great student in high school and you are fighting to do well in college. Your note-taking skills are weak. You know that you missed some important information that will be on the quiz. A has good notes, so you borrowed them for the night. When you started to review A's notes you found that he/she had over 60 pages of outlined material, plus a few diagrams. The more you look over the notes, the more you realize how much you don't understand. Photocopying the notes would take valuable time and money (and you are in a panic by now), so you make up the excuse that you are sick, tell your neighbor to pass the word, forget about A, and start cramming for the quiz.

2. The Cafeteria

Student C: You are standing in line waiting to discover the mystery food of the day, when you notice that some upperclassmen, wearing similar jackets, are letting their friends in line ahead of you. You can understand letting one friend join another for lunch. But if the trend continues you will be moving backward. Your next class is not for another hour, so time pressure does not concern you. You are, however, outraged at the blatant disregard the upperclassmen are showing for the rest of the students in line—including you. You saw this same situation take place last week and once the week before, but this is the first time you are behind this group. You want to say something. What should you say and to whom?

Student D: You are a pledge in a social fraternity/sorority who has been ordered by the upperclass members of your organization to get to the cafeteria early and secure a place in line for them. You know you are being placed in a socially awkward situation which tests your loyalty to the group. You want to succeed at pledging very much and are willing to take responsibility for your actions. You are also a bit embarrassed at how many of your upperclass members are cutting in line, but the rewards of acceptance have been worth it in the past few weeks.

Note: The third person in your small group can role-play the part of the upperclassmen or anyone else you elect him/her to be for the purpose of the role-play.

3. The Library

Student E: You study in the main room of the library regularly between your classes. You prefer the library because it is quiet and you are more easily distracted elsewhere. Midterm exams are coming soon. The library is filling up with a lot of students who are "studying together," which seems to require talking and laughing at times. You are distracted and irritated that these newcomers do not observe the quiet rules. F and some friends are sitting at the next table. They have not opened their books. F is relating a story about a party last weekend which is quite hilarious. You find yourself laughing a bit but also upset that you have been distracted from your studying.

Student F: You are a fairly good student who has plenty of time to study in the evening. Some classmates suggested that you all go to the library to compare notes before studying for the midterm. When you get a table in the library, the normal discussion begins with the expectation on your part that you will begin to study in a few minutes. There seem to be a lot of students talking in the main room of the library, so you do not feel that you are really disturbing anyone, and that if someone couldn't study there, he/she could always go to one of the quieter places on another floor.

4. The Roommate

Student G: When you and your roommate moved in eight weeks ago, you hit it off. You went places together, had a few classes to- gether, studied together, and went to a few parties together. In short, you became friends quickly. Because you got along so well in the beginning, neither of you saw a reason to negotiate rules for the room. Now your roommate, H, has joined up with another group of friends whom you don't feel quite comfortable with. H's new friends stop by several times a week and stay for a few hours—usually when you have work to do. At first they asked whether they were disturbing you and, to be nice, you said: "Oh no, it's OK." Now you are sorry that you practically invited them in, but you still want to be polite to them because you don't want to disrupt the relationship you have with your roommate.

Student H: You are glad that you have your roommate instead of some antisocial nerd. You get along well with each other and with each other's friends. At first you were concerned that your room- mate, G, would not like some of your new friends. Now you are happy to see that you can all be together several times a week with everybody doing his own thing.

5. The Professor

Professor I: You have been teaching at the college eight years and have been told that the students like your classes. You demand that your students hand in their term papers on time, neatly typed without typing errors. At times you may appear to be tough on some of them, but you feel you are preparing them for the world after college, which is much less forgiving than the classroom. When J turned in a paper that was hand-printed a day late, you graded him/her down one letter grade and wrote on the paper that you were generous for looking at it at all.

Student J: You are working your way through school with little money to spare. You could not afford a typist or a typewriter. Compared to the other students you feel like the poor kid in town. And you feel a bit backward, because many of the students seem to be using computers to word-process their papers. You believe that you wrote a good paper. The ideas were clear and well researched. And you stayed up for hours printing it neatly by hand to make up for not typing it. You resent the fact that your paper was graded down because it was not typed and it was a day late. However, you feel that you must tell Professor I that you did your best with what you have.

6. The Cheaters

Student K: You are an average student in a tough program, where the material is difficult and the competition is stiff. You have always studied hard and have just gotten by on the exams. You are now in a large required course, which is used by the department to weed out the weaker students from the major. One group of students has a file of the old exams from this course. In addition, they have sat in the back of the room and compared answers during the quizzes and the midterm. Their scores have been high. Because the class is graded on a curve, you feel that you could fail the class because their cheating is affecting the grading scale. You don't really want to start trouble with this group, because you may be with them for three more years. You don't want to be known as the class tattletale. And it is not clear to you whether the professor doesn't care or is just unaware of the cheating.

Professor L: You have been teaching this course for several years. Somebody in the department has to teach the "hurdle class" and, as the junior member, it was left to you. The size of the class makes it unmanageable. You do not know the students. The exams are graded by computer. From time to time you have heard from other students that some students are cheating in your class. You cannot do anything about it without hard proof. One student against another will not hold up in the campus judicial process. You figure the cheaters will get their due some day and have left the matter at that.

Note: The third person in your small group can role-play one of the cheaters or anyone else that you elect him/her to be for the purpose of this role-play.

Closure: You should have found that role-plays can be fun if you just let yourself go. This is about the most effective way to learn a new behavior, because we learn best by doing. Also, in role-plays you don't have anything to lose.

Journal Entry

You have just been magically changed into an assertive person. Write a short story on the topic of how you were changed and what effect the change had on your life.

This Author's Assertive Answers to the Questionnaire

1. No. I openly point out how I feel that the person is being unfair.
2. No. Sometimes it is best to argue openly and honestly with another in order to clear the air and settle the issue.
3. No. If I do accidentally say the wrong thing to someone, I can always apologize.
4. Yes. If I hide my feelings, they will only grow and come out in another form of aggression later.
5. Yes. We would first have to negotiate how we would like to live. Then each would be justified in insisting that the other live up to the agreement.
6. Yes. Of course there are special cases, such as the elderly and infirm, or perhaps someone with a crying infant .
7. No. There is no reason to be nervous around others.
8. No. If I knew he/she was short of cash, I would not ask. If he/she had it and I was in need—what are friends for if not to help each other?
9. Yes. I feel that a person should pay his/her debts.
10. No. A little teasing among friends is a form of play. Too much is a form of aggression in which I do not feel a desire to participate.
11. No. There are almost always seats in the front. If I move quickly so as to consider the view of others, no one should feel offended.
12. Yes.
13. Yes. If a friend was having a problem, I would try to help. But if he/she began to abuse our friendship, I would call it to his/her attention.
14. Yes. Eye contact is very useful for the first time. If the interrupter does not get the message, then saying, "Excuse me, I was talking" will usually work.
15. Yes. If I am paying for the service, I expect to get it.

16. Yes. If the landlord is willing to take my money, I feel he/she should be willing to comply with the rest of the bargain.
17. Yes. Everyone is entitled to get what he/she pays for.
18. Yes. I might begin by questioning his/her position in order to discover whether he/she knows something that I don't.
19. Yes. If I said yes, either I would be frustrated attempting to meet the unreasonable request or they would be disappointed at the results.
20. Yes.

❖ Chapter 21 ❖

Managing Your Finances at College

In *College Is Only the Beginning*, Ray Edwards gives you sound advice on organizing and managing the financial aspects of student life. The main purpose of this chapter is to give you the worksheets that make the organizing part easy—just fill in the blanks. The managing part is a little harder. You must take control of your money and not spend it all in the first month or two of the academic year. I can't tell you how many times students have told me that in the first lonesome days away at college they spent hours on long-distance calls, only to live like paupers for the next two months. This brings us to the second purpose of this chapter: discovering the spending traps. Group Activity 21.1 will help you become aware of how money can burn a hole in your pocket.

Using the Financial Planner System

Three worksheets are supplied for your use in this chapter. Worksheet 21.2A should be used to record your expenses as they occur. Make a photocopy for additional weeks before you begin recording. At the beginning of each month, enter your budget per item on worksheet 21.2B. At the end of each month, enter your expenses in the "reality" column of worksheet 21.2B. Then compare budget with reality to see how well you were able to control your finances. Worksheet 21.2C should be used to help you predict your yearly expenses and plan on ways of finding the funds to meet them.

Group Activity 21.1 *Student Spending Traps and Tips*

Purpose: Your new campus world presents you with many opportunities to spend your money. Although some purchases are worth making if you can afford them, others might be temptations worth avoiding. Each campus has its unique spending traps. Find yours early, spend wisely, and your money will go farther. This activity will help you discover spending traps, find discount prices, and obtain some advice on how to find extra spending money.

Directions: Ask two upperclassmen to complete the following questions. When your interviews are completed, designate one student in your seminar to be the editor for each of the five responses. Each seminar member should give his/her interview responses to the appropriate editor. The editors should be given about a week to compile the responses into a booklet of student finance tips. This booklet could be combined with similar booklets from other seminars and reproduced by the student newspaper or student government, posted, or put on reserve in the library for others to review or copy.

Student Spending Questionnaire

1. When I realized how much money I spent on (*note two different student responses*)

_____ , I was shocked.

2. The best place to find discount prices for personal items is:

_____

_____

_____

3. The best way to save money on books and supplies is:

_____

_____

_____

4. The best way to earn some extra spending money at college is:

_____

_____

_____

5. The best information on student loans and financial aid can be found:

_____

_____

_____

Closure: Combining information from the experience of consumers is the best way to find the most economical path through your academic years. If you are not a good money manager, ask advice from those who manage well. You will find yourself thinking differently about spending responsibly.

Journal Entry

Most of us are guilty of impulse buying—sometimes to the detriment of our health, in cases such as purchases of cigarettes, junk food, and alcohol. Most often our impulse buying makes us owners of more than we need or can use. Write a description of what went on inside you when you made your last impulse purchase. Then place yourself in your most typical impulse purchase situation (for example, the candy counter). While standing there, write a description of everything that attracts you to the item. List all the reasons you should not purchase the item. When you return to your room, confess to your journal whether you purchased or resisted and why.

Expense Record for Two Weeks 21.2A

Expenses	Sun	Mon	Tue	Wed	Thu	Fri	Sat	Sun	Mon	Tue	Wed	Thu	Fri	Sat	Subtotal/item
Educational expenses															
Housing/rent															
Board/food															
Personal															
Transportation															
Parking															
Laundry															
Clothing															
Telephone															
Entertainment															
Recreation															
Vehicle															
Insurance															
Other															
Subtotal/day															Total

Monthly Financial Planner 21.2B

Expenses	Budget	Reality	Budget	Reality
Educational Expenses				
Tuition				
Fees				
Books				
Supplies				
Other				
Subtotal				
Living Expenses				
Housing (rent)				
Board (food)				
Personal				
Transportation				
Laundry				
Clothes				
Telephone				
Entertainment				
Other				
Subtotal				
Total				
Difference +/−				

Academic Year Financial Planner 21.2C

Expenses	First Term	Second Term	Resources

Educational Expenses

			A. Savings
Tuition			Yours $ _____
Fees			Parents $ _____
Books			B. Family
Supplies			Cash $ _____
Other			Loans $ _____
Subtotal			C. Work

Living Expenses

			Summer $ _____
			Part-time $ _____
Housing (rent)			D. Benefits
Board (food)			Social Sec. $ _____
Personal			Other $ _____
Transportation			E. Financial Aid
Laundry			Fed. Grant $ _____
Clothes			Stud. Loan $ _____
Telephone			Scholarship $ _____
Entertainment			F. Other $ _____
Other			$ _____
Subtotal			

Total			
Annual Total			**Total** $ _____

❖ Chapter 22 ❖

The Returning Student Success Steps

In *College Is Only the Beginning*, Dorothy Fidler gives some sound advice to the "returning student"—the person who either comes back to college or starts college after the age of 25. Feelings of anxiety, inadequacy, and confusion are common among these older students. Fidler suggests that returning students will be in better control of these feelings if they label them "challenging excitement" rather than "apprehension." In addition, I have also found that a solid understanding of one's own reality can be a sure cure for a case of anxiety and confusion.

Too often people return to college without examining their dislikes, weaknesses, and avoidances (including unconscious avoidances) as well as their likes, skills, strengths, and motivations. People feel confusion when they do not know what decision to make at a new crossroad in life. Many students return to college because they feel a need to get something more out of life. They are looking for fulfillment. Others return for a course or two to advance their careers. Launching on a midlife quest for satisfaction carries less certainty with it than returning to college to pick up a few courses for a certification or a job promotion.

This chapter is designed to assist the returning student who is heading for a change in his or her life—the student who has returned to college to improve himself or herself, to earn more money, and to enjoy life more. Before you continue with these exercises and activities, you should be sure to complete the study skills assessment in Chapter 5 and "Your Personality/Your Career" in Chapter 9. Most students improve their performance after some instruction in study skills. For returning students, study skills courses or workshops can be crucial to their success and should be considered.

With the feedback from these exercises and some personal reflection, you can begin to make an inventory of your assets before building on them.

Individual Exercise 22.1 *A Quick Look at What You Want*

Purpose: Few people can define what they want when questioned. These same people can tell you exactly what they don't like based on their past experience. This exercise is designed to help you define what you don't want and what you do want.

Directions: In the space provided in Charts 22.1A and 22.1B, write in the words that best describe the item or experience indicated.

Life Preference Chart 22.1A

Category	What You Don't Want	What You Do Want

Family

What You Don't Want	What You Do Want
Your worst experience:	Your best experience:
Parents/support/authority:	Parents/support/authority:
Spouse/support/cooperation:	Spouse/support/cooperation:
Children/care/responsibilities:	Children/care/responsibilities:

Financial concerns

What You Don't Want	What You Do Want
Your worst experience:	Your best experience:
Needs that are unmet:	Needs that are met:
Responsibilities unmet:	Responsibilities met:
Desires that are unmet:	Desires that are met:

Natural skills

What You Don't Want	What You Do Want
Your worst embarrassment:	Your best experience:
Physical skill:	Physical skill:
Mental skill:	Mental skill:
Emotional skill:	Emotional skill:
Social skill:	Social skill:
Learning skill:	Learning skill:

Self-image

What You Don't Want	What You Do Want
State your weakest area and how you can best improve it.	State your strongest area and how you can best build on it.

Life Preference Chart 22.1B

Category	Negative	Positive

Residence

Your worst experience:	Your best experience:
Building:	Building:
Roommates:	Roommates:
Neighbors:	Neighbors:
Geographical area:	Geographical area:

Coworkers

Your worst experience:	Your best experience:
Large group:	Large group:
Small group:	Small group:
Values demonstrated by least liked:	Values demonstrated by best liked:

Employment or Volunteer Experience

Your worst experience:	Your best experience:
Early job:	Early job:
Best paying:	Best paying:
Volunteer:	Volunteer:

Lifestyle

Your worst experience:	Your best experience:
One that you have seen or heard of:	One that you have seen or heard of:

Goals

Things you have never cared about or never finished:	Things you always care about and love to work toward:

Closure: The first step in establishing a clear, positive direction is the completion of a life review and a skills and values assessment. This exercise, as well as the study skills assessment in Chapter 5 and "Your Personality/Your Career" in Chapter 9, should help you set the stage for the following life review exercise and activity.

Individual Exercise 22.2 *Listing Priorities*

Purpose: If you do not establish priorities in your busy life, you will increase your stress potential to the point of illness, as Fidler observed. Nobody can do two things at once. Order your priorities and do one thing at a time. Your college success and your health depend on it.

Directions: Here is a partial list of things most people do each day at some point in their lives. In Column 1 of Chart 22.2A write in the items that are priorities in your life now that you are a returning student. Assign a priority number to each item, along with the number of hours that are required for you to attend to the priority. Then place the number of the priority and the hours in the box for its day(s) in your week. Adjust your list until you have enough time to get some recreation or exercise and sleep every day. Use the time management form in Chapter 5 to organize your days on paper.

Some Possible Priorities

two or three hours study time/credit

commuting

employment

spouse

children

friends

parents

recreation

laundry

class time

other

volunteer work

food preparation

food shopping

eating

house cleaning

house maintenance

exercise

bill paying

religious event

errands

other

Priority Chart 22.2A

Priority	Hours each time	Times per week												

	Mon priority/hrs.	Tue priority/hrs.	Wed priority/hrs.	Thu priority/hrs.	Fri priority/hrs.	Sat priority/hrs.	Sun priority/hrs.
	total hrs.	total hrs.	total hrs.	total hrs.	total hrs.	total hrs.	total hrs.

Things that you need help with

People/agencies who can help

Individual Exercise 22.3 *The Life Review*

Purpose: It is important to know yourself—your past experience and the meaning of that experience to you at this time in your life. This exercise, together with Group Activity 22.4, is designed to give you a better understanding of who you are and how you can best pursue a successful future in your social world.

Directions: The general rule of the life review is that the older you are, the longer the review process is and the more fulfilling it can be. If you have not been a reflective person, you can expect to spend more time on this assignment and get proportionally more out of it. Many people write several hundred pages and enjoy it so much they talk about it for years. You and your instructor should determine the length of time you should give to this assignment, with the understanding that some people may want to work on it for a year or more.

Acquire a loose-leaf binder and insert at least one page for each year that you have lived. Number the pages 1 to your present age and follow the process below. Add paper as needed during the assignment.

Life Review Process

1. On the appropriate pages write your milestone events. Under each milestone title, write an explorative essay, story, poem, or drawing that expresses the following: **(a)** your motivations and other social forces and natural causes that brought about the event; **(b)** how you felt about the event at the time; **(c)** the impact the event had on your life's path; and **(d)** how you feel about the event now.
2. Insert a new piece of paper after each essay or poem and list the new physical, mental, emotional, social, and learning skills you acquired because of the milestone event.
3. Make a separate list of all the hobbies you ever had. Locate them in your review book in the appropriate year of your initial interest and be sure to write about: **(a)** why you were first interested in this hobby; **(b)** the extent of your interest; **(c)** how far the hobby extended your social network (people that you know or know of); and **(d)** the physical, mental, emotional, social, and learning skills you gained through the hobby.

Group Activity 22.4 *Discussing Your Review*

Purpose: After you get the basic outline of each milestone event, you are ready to explore new levels of meaning. Sharing experiences with other adults is one of the truly enriching experiences of life. Discussing milestones may be the greatest self-indulgent pleasure of your life. It will give you the rare (in our culture) opportunity to set aside competitiveness and materialism and explore the truly human side of your existence. The insights you gain into your own complex makeup will guide you in your decision.

Directions: Discuss the review process with some other returning students, faculty, and advisers. Invite those you feel comfortable with to join you in an informal milestone discussion group once a week. Five members is a good number for a group. Permission of the other members should always be obtained before inviting a new member or guest. All discussions should avoid value judgments, unless explicitly requested by the reviewer. The main function of the group should be to contribute additional observations about skills gained and personality strengths observed.

Closure: A life review is a process that you should undergo as part of planning a change in your direction. Your new goals and objectives must grow out of your past or you will never feel comfortable with the new you.

Journal Entry

Write an essay describing the difference between what the college experience means to you and how you perceive the freshman experience of the "traditional-age students."

❖ Chapter 23 ❖

Closure

Your education will take you to new and untold places if you immerse yourself in knowledge. I often travel backward to visit the origins of humanity—to a time before factories and work-days; a time before anyone knew what time it was. When I look into my life and the lives unfolding around me, I wrest a few moments from the work world to watch us growing together. At that moment I touch life and it touches me. And then I move on—renewed, centered, and energized—with the conviction that I am on the right path: my path. I invite you to do the same in my "Return to the Fire."

Keep in touch.

Return to the Fire

Strip away the glitter world
dissolve the buildings round
mirrored glass, golden brass, and stereophonic sound
unplug, tune out, take the exit lane—
distill life to its essence
to make your stay here sane

Distant sight—untold delight
from ages gone away
journey there—become aware
from fixed present stray—
and know that life from then
to now affects your every day

Oh that content in my mind
handed down from distant time
a spark from dance drum word to soul
grows from dream to act to player's role

And there sit I upon the stage
'tween life and death—a turning page
I bend and bow and tribute pay
to the god of work who maims each day

Even as a child I knew
that workdays numbered five
then there were two just set aside
to play and dance and THRIVE

But now the work goes day and night
my Giant Eagle[1] soars
with sell cell sell and by buy bye
which somehow gives us more

Oh Edison! Turn out your light and
let my people sleep
rest the content of our minds
so we can journey deep

[1]Giant Eagle is a large supermarket near the author—the first to stay open 24 hours and prosper as a innovator.

Give us cause to burn a fire
release the sun at night!
hisssss crackle snap and sizzzzzzzle log
and then another ad
form and rule with
must and should drift up
as first match to calendar to kindle
log ignite!

And There! we break free and
soar on timeless wing sing
wind to rhyme through time
dream dream—undream machines

Melt perfect bombs and guns
let passions rage as they must
but not to dust—not *all* to dust!
let single hearts and single dreams
take us where we have not seen
and try and risk and fail but not
fail to grow as souls not products
grow—

Evolve as child gives birth to
youth unmeasured—except by sun's cycle
and moon's rise—by seasons
not reasons—not reasons to grow
except to grow—to take root in a well-
suited clime and gather in and take on
and grow strong—flourishing in the
noonday sun heat of life as all
our million parents did in their
timeless age—an age time clockless
except for ours

Life's center bursts forth Expression
Passion Love and tender care joy
of giving received—that time handed
down to hand—seized in day and
reflected in the deep inner pool of night
where fears and myths are born behind
closed eye and felt deep—soul rooted

Let not dawn to alarm
to shift quick caffeine to boil
to toil only to foil slow reflective rise
not to time one's departure from myth with
buzzzzzz CLANG Ring
stop that thing toss it out! and let
your inner self rise slow
beam gleam shine and shout

I'M ALIVE I'M ALIVE

Breathe deep and share the air that
cycled through a line of lungs linked
to chain of life through leaves and
sea—dinosaur to car exhaust
                    don't exhaust

BE ALIVE !